Twayne's United States Authors Series

EDITOR OF THIS VOLUME
Kenneth Eble
University of Utah

Charles A. Siringo

TUSAS 376

Charles A. Siringo

CHARLES A. SIRINGO

By ORLAN SAWEY

TWAYNE PUBLISHERS

A DIVISION OF G. K. HALL & CO., BOSTON

Published in 1981 by Twayne Publishers,
A Division of G. K. Hall & Co.
All Rights Reserved

Printed on permanent/durable acid-free paper and bound
in the United States of America

First Printing

Frontispiece drawing by Nina Sawey

Library of Congress Cataloging in Publication Data

Sawey, Orlan, 1920 -
Charles A. Siringo.

(Twayne's United States authors series ; TUSAS 376)
Bibliography: p. 152 - 57
Includes index.
1.   Siringo, Charles A., 1855 - 1928.   2.   The West—
History—1848 - 1950.   3.   Frontier and pioneer life—The
West.   4.   Historians—The West—Biography.   5.   Cow-
boys—The West—Biography.
F595.S62S28   978'.02'0924 [B]   80-19602
ISBN 0-8057-7312-6

To the late Frances Alexander,
who introduced me to the literature of the Southwest,
and to the late Mody C. Boatright,
who encouraged me in its study.

Contents

About the Author

Orlan Sawey retired at Texas A&I University in 1977, having taught English for thirty-one years in colleges and universities in Texas, Arkansas, Tennessee, Virginia, and North Carolina. His chief interest is American literature and folklore, with special emphasis on Southwestern and Western literature. His graduate theses at the University of Texas were on cowboy autobiographical writing, under the supervision of the late Mody C. Boatright. In 1969 his *Bernard DeVoto* was published in the Twayne United States Authors series; he and his wife, Nina, have edited the reminiscences of Hettie Lee Ewing (privately printed); and he has published articles in several areas.

Mr. Sawey now lives at Bryson City, North Carolina.

Preface

"Who is Charlie Siringo?" This is the question that arose most frequently as I talked about this book to my friends. My answer usually was that Siringo was a well-known figure in the cattleman's West—he was the first cowboy to publish an autobiography—and that he deserves to be better known. During the last ten years his name has appeared frequently in Western movies and TV programs dealing with the bad men of the West, although little real information is given about the man and his work. The purpose of this book is to supply that which is lacking in the presentations of the media.

Although Siringo did not believe that there was such a person as a "typical cowboy"—as one old-time cowboy put it, "We is all just bowlegged humans"—his life, like the lives of thousands of his contemporaries, coincided with the beginnings, rise, development, and end of the Range Cattle Industry, before the advent of barbed wire, in the (possibly) good old free days. In 1883, when change was imminent, he quit cowboy life and eventually (in 1886) became a Pinkerton detective. For the rest of his active life he was a "cowboy detective" involved in most of the violent activities of a changing West that was disturbed by the end of the open range and the development of new social institutions, such as the labor unions.

Siringo was different from most of his contemporaries in that he wrote at length about his experiences, in an obvious attempt to explain what had happened in the West.

In considering how to present in his first book his ideas on the life of the old - time cowboy, Siringo finally decided that the best way was to tell of his own "short and sweet" life. His books are, I believe, the best interpretations yet published of the life of the cowboy as it was between 1865 and 1885, the open range period. Also, he saw and described much of the violence prevalent on the Western frontier from 1885 to 1910, an excessively violent era.

In an effort to analyze and explain Charley Siringo's writing, I chose to study his books in the framework of his life, to present the facts of that "short and sweet" life that were the basis of his writing.

My method has been to examine critically his works as frontier chronicles, the interpretation of a shrewd (but not academically systematic) mind of the developments in Western life which have stirred the imaginations of millions of Americans. I have made no attempts to analyze systematically the myths about the cowboy and the cowboy bad man; Siringo, a man of action, was seldom analytical or systematic. I have tried, rather, to present Siringo's story, critically examining the facts as he presented them.

Some criticism is necessary, and I have made critical evaluations, for the most part, in discussing Siringo's books as they tell the interesting story of Siringo's West. Also, I have presented a final evaluation, mine and that of others, in the last chapter.

Hundreds of Siringo's contemporaries, cowboys who worked during the open - range period, thought that the events of their youth were important enough to record. Nobody has been able to explain adequately the reason cowboy life inspired such chronicles, when farming, mining, sheepherding, or the other Western occupations of the last quarter of the nineteeth century were not equally inspiring. The cowboy autobiography has made a considerable contribution to the history of the Old West, although frequently in attempting to explain the myths of the cattle industry cowboy writers have added to the myths. And historians and literary men, most of whom are romanticists with imaginary saddle burns, have not done so well in explaining the myth of the American cowboy. Siringo was the first and probably the best of the cowboy autobiographers. Events in his life illustrate vividly the events of an important era in the development of the West.

ORLAN SAWEY

Texas A&I University

Chronology

1855   Birth on February 7, in the "Dutch Settlement," Matagorda Peninsula, Texas; son of immigrants, Italian father and Irish mother.

1867   First work as a cowboy, age eleven.

1870   Return to Texas after two years' stay in Illinois and New Orleans.

1871   Employment as a cowboy on "Shanghai" Pierce's Rancho Grande.

1876   Trip up Chisholm Trail with W. B. Grimes herd.

1877   Trip up the trail again and with group which established the LX Ranch in the Texas Panhandle. Cowboy for the LX until 1883.

1880— Involvement with some of the Lincoln County, New Mex-
1881   ico, troubles with Billy the Kid.

1883   Early in March, marriage to Mamie Lloyd at Caldwell, Kansas. Separation from LX Ranch in September to become owner of ice cream and cigar store in Caldwell.

1885   First edition of *A Texas Cow Boy.*

1886   Second edition of *A Texas Cow Boy.* Beginning of work as a detective for Pinkerton's National Detective Agency, in Chicago. Transfer to Denver in the fall, where he worked as "cowboy detective."

1889   Death of Mamie Lloyd Siringo in Denver.

1890s Marriage to Lillie Thomas, Denver; separation "soon after."

1907   Resignation from Pinkerton's and removal to Sunny Slope Ranch, Santa Fe. Free-lance detective until 1916.

1912   *A Cowboy Detective.*

1915   *Two Evil Isms.*

1919   *A Lone Star Cowboy* and *A Song Companion to A Lone Star Cowboy.*

1920   *History of "Billy the Kid."*

1922   Removal to San Diego, California, then to Los Angeles and Hollywood.

1927   Publication of *Riata and Spurs*, original and revised editions.

1928   Death in Hollywood, California, October 18.

CHAPTER 1

Cowboy Chronicler and His Works

CHARLES Angelo Siringo was born on February 7, 1855, at the "Dutch Settlement" on Matagorda Peninsula on the Gulf Coast of Texas. His father was an Italian immigrant, and his mother, Bridgit, was born in Ireland. "Am I not a queer conglomerate," wrote Siringo, "a sweet-scented mixture indeed!"[1]

Although Matagorda Peninsula might accurately be said to be in the "extreme southern part" of Texas (this was Siringo's description), it is more than two hundred miles north of the "extreme tip" of Texas, as another writer interpreted Siringo's words.[2] In fact, the peninsula is just outside the diamond-shaped area which Walter Prescott Webb indicated was the cradle of what he called the Cattle Kingdom, an area bounded by San Antonio on the north, Brownsville on the south, Old Indianola on the east, and Laredo on the west.[3] Webb's boundaries, approximate as they are, do not belie Siringo's statement that he was "born and brought up amidst wild, long-horn cattle and mustangs."[4] Wild cattle roamed the peninsula, and early in his life, Siringo, whose mother, according to the 1860 census reports, unprophetically called him Angelo, saw "crowds of Cow Boys" come to the peninsula from the mainland to rope wild steers.[5] The Gulf Coast area between Corpus Christi and Houston, "Shanghai" Pierce country, was better cattle country than the brush country to the west because the rainfall was heavier.

Siringo, then, began his life in the area where Webb's Cattle Kingdom (E. E. Dale's Range Cattle Industry) developed. He was on hand when, as a result of the trail drives and other events, the industry spread to the Panhandle of Texas and to the Northern Plains states. He quit working as a cowboy about the same time that the open range was no longer a factor in the development of ranching. He was a "cowboy detective" during the period of violence which marked the end of the American frontier. He wrote, for the most

13

part, autobiographies, chronological in order and sparse in exposi-
tion. Except for part of one book and two pamphlets, he wrote
about what happened to Siringo.

His approach, however, was not without logic. The beginnings,
developments, and maturity of Charlie Siringo paralleled the beginnings, development, and maturity of the Range Cattle Industry.
The personal conflicts of Siringo, caused by the end of the supposedly free, untrammeled existence of the cowboy, motivated his
continuous effort both to explain the past and to justify his more
than twenty years as a Pinkerton detective. He was a part of life on
the open range and of the violence which marked its end. He had
only one story to tell, that of Charlie Siringo, cowboy. He believed
that the story of his life illustrated "the environment of these young
cowboys throughout the State of Texas from whence sprang the first
cowboys."[6]

Siringo began writing his life story relatively early and published
his last autobiographical work less than two years before his death.
According to his tongue-in-cheek preface to *A Texas Cow Boy*,
Siringo first began thinking of writing a book during the winter of
1882 - 1883; he gave as an excuse for writing the book "money—
and lots of it."[7]

The first, and probably the best, book by Siringo was published
in Chicago by M. Umbdenstock and Company, 1885, while Siringo
was still the Cigar King merchant of Caldwell, Kansas. He had quit
work as a cowboy in September 1883. The title page of the first edition gives the flavor of the book:

A TEXAS COW BOY, OR, FIFTEEN YEARS ON THE HURRICANE
DECK OF A SPANISH PONY. TAKEN FROM REAL LIFE, BY CHAS.
A. SIRINGO, AN OLD STOVE UP "COW PUNCHER," WHO HAS
SPENT NEARLY TWENTY YEARS ON THE GREAT WESTERN CAT-
TLE RANCHES.

It might be noted that the old stove-up cow puncher finished the
book before he was thirty.

The first edition, now very rare, was a well-printed, well-bound
volume. It must have sold well, because Siringo brought out a new
edition the next year (Siringo and Dobson, Chicago, publishers),
with a thirty-page "Addenda," a tongue-in-cheek essay on how to
get rich quick in the West, how the tenderfoot cowboy mistreated

his horse, and how the absentee owners would lose their shirts in the cold winter of 1885 - 1886.

The book remained in print in various editions, mainly paperback, until 1926. In the preface to *A Lone Star Cowboy*, published in 1919 by Siringo, the author stated that *A Texas Cow Boy* [the spelling is his] had sold nearly a million copies. J. Frank Dobie, in the 1950 reprint of *A Texas Cow Boy*, indicated that Siringo had exaggerated the total.[8]

Siringo's second book, *A Cowboy Detective*, 1912, which was in print until about 1924, traces Siringo's life from 1886, when he began working as the cowboy operative for Pinkerton's National Detective Agency, until 1907, when he quit Pinkerton's. In the book, censored because of conflict with Pinkerton's, he calls the agency "Dickenson's" and gives most of the characters in the book fictitious names.

Siringo's next book, *Two Evil Isms: Pinkertonism and Anarchism* (1915), gives some of the details of his struggle with Pinkerton's about the publication of *A Cowboy Detective*, which was kept from being published for two years by Pinkerton's and was finally published in a censored form. Probably all of the details will never be known, although Charles D. Peavy, in his introduction to the facsimile reproduction of *Two Evil Isms* (1967) and in his pamphlet, *Charles A. Siringo, A Texas Picaro*, has explored many of the details. *Two Evil Isms* summarizes much of the material in *A Cowboy Detective*, but essentially, as the title indicates, it is a diatribe against the Pinkerton's National Detective Agency.

Siringo's next book, privately printed in 1919, was *A Lone Star Cowboy*. On the title page, under a double line separating it from the title, the following information appears (Siringo was fond of long subtitles):

Being fifty years experience in the saddle as Cowboy, Detective and New Mexico Ranger, on every cow trail in the wooly [sic] old west. Also the doings of some "bad" cowboys, such as "Billy the Kid," Wess Harding [sic] and "Kid Curry". By CHAS. A. SIRINGO Author of "Fifteen Years on the Hurricane Deck of a Spanish Pony" and "A Cowboy Detective." Santa Fe, New Mexico, 1919.

The first 214 pages of *A Lone Star Cow Boy* are a rewriting of *A Texas Cow Boy*, with the style toned down somewhat but the violent incidents played up, possibly because the passing of time permitted him to be more frank or, a less generous interpretation, possibly because violence had become a dominant theme in writing about the West. The rest of the book, sixty-five pages, deals with his life as a merchant in Caldwell, Kansas, the opening of Oklahoma to settlement, a brief mention of his twenty-two years of service with Pinkerton's, his pursuit of a man who he thought was "Kid Curry" for the William J. Burns Detective Agency, a visit to the Gulf Coast country of his youth, a fairly accurate account of the establishment and use of the Chisholm Trail, and an account of his two years' service as a New Mexico Ranger.

In my opinion, *A Lone Star Cow Boy* is not as good a book as *A Texas Cow Boy*, his best, although the book gives information about Siringo not found elsewhere (for example, a short account of his marriage to Lillie Thomas and the birth of a son, Lee Roy, who later became a banker in Southern California).[9] (I received a letter from Lee Roy Siringo in 1947 stating that his father's papers had been burned by mistake by a family that had rented his home.) The chief defect of *A Lone Star Cowboy* is that someone evidently edited the style to make it more "correct," although the editor did not teach him how to spell "woolly" (see above). This is also, I believe, the chief defect of *Riata and Spurs*, Siringo's last book.

The same year that *A Lone Star Cowboy* was published, Siringo also printed a forty-two page pamphlet, *A Song Companion to A Lone Star Cowboy*. The title page carries the following subtitle: "Old Favorite Cow-Camp Songs." The price was 35 cents; it was published in Santa Fe, New Mexico, with the copyright date being 1919. J. Frank Dobie, in his bibliography to the 1950 edition of *A Texas Cow Boy*, rightly calls it "a shoddy collection."

In 1920 Siringo privately published a slight book entitled *History of "Billy the Kid"*. Siringo was still fond of long title pages: the rest of the title page reads as follows:

The true life of the most daring young outlaw of the age.
He was the leading spirit in the bloody Lincoln County, New Mexico, war. When a bullet from Sheriff Pat Garrett's pistol pierced his breast he was only twenty-one years of age, and had killed twenty-one men, not counting Indians. His six years of daring outlawry has never been equalled in the annals of criminal history. By CHAS. A. SIRINGO. Author of: "Fifteen Years on the Hurricane Deck of a Spanish Pony," "A Cowboy Detective," and "A Lone Star Cowboy".

The book adds little to the account in *A Texas Cow Boy*, and it is based, as were most accounts prior to 1960, on Pat Garrett's book on Billy the Kid, which was probably written by newspaperman Ash Upson to build up the reputation of Garrett. Iconoclastic historians have shown that much of the Billy the Kid legend is merely legend—but the real story has been printed elsewhere.[10] Siringo cast little light on the Kid's life; he merely rehashed what had already been recorded.

The only book by Siringo published by a national publisher is *Riata and Spurs*, brought out by the Houghton Mifflin Company in 1927. The subtitle is one of Siringo's shorter ones: "The Story of a Lifetime spent in the Saddle as a Cowboy and Detective." The publication history of *Riata and Spurs* is unique. The first 119 pages of the first printing are another revision, with more "errors" edited out, of *A Texas Cow Boy*. Pages 120 - 268 are a revision of *A Cowboy Detective*, with original names restored, including that of Pinkerton's National Detective Agency. But something happened. Charles D. Peavy correctly says that the detective agency intimidated Houghton Mifflin into deleting pages 120 - 208 and substituting material originally intended to be included in a manuscript entitled "The Bad Men Cowboys." Peavy states, too hastily, that neither Houghton Mifflin nor the Pinkerton archives could provide any information on the reasons for the changes.[11]

Siringo's own acount provides a little more light. In 1925 Siringo had submitted a manuscript entitled "Bad Man Cowboys of the Early West" to "a New York Publisher." In September 1927 he wrote that the Pinkertons "put a stop" to Houghton Mifflin's publishing *Riata and Spurs* on the grounds that he had "Exposed Secrets of the Agency." Material had been taken from the "Bad Man Cowboys" manuscript, he said, and had been substituted for the Pinkerton material. Siringo wrote that Houghton Mifflin had indicated the revised book would be better than the original. "Hope so," Siringo wrote. On September 14, 1927, the revised book had already gone to press.[12] A full account of Houghton Mifflin's losing struggle with the agency is in Chapter 7, below.

To the casual observer, the revised printing does not seem different from the original. A careful observation will note, however, that the subtitle was changed from the original, above, to "The Story of a Lifetime Spent in the Saddle as Cowboy and *Ranger*" [emphasis mine].

One collector of Western books assures me that the revised edition is harder to find than the original. The newer edition, however, must have had more than one printing, since I have seen a copy dated 1928 and another dated 1931. But Houghton Mifflin's not indicating that later printings had been revised is strange; the omission, I am sure, has led to some confusion.

In March 1948 a well-known writer of Westerns ran an advertisement in the *New York Times Book Review* asking for information about a Siringo book, not *Riata and Spurs* or *Two Evil Isms*. The book, she said, dealt with Siringo's Pinkerton experiences; it was an expansion of *A Cowboy Detective*. She had read the first edition of *Riata and Spurs* and then was puzzled about not being able to find the same material on rereading the book, obviously the revised edition.[13]

Which *Riata and Spurs* is the real one? That depends on what the reader wants. The first edition is in my opinion the only volume which gives any real information about how the Pinkertons operated (Horan's books, authorized and approved by the agency, are varnished accounts); Siringo's book spurred them to a reaction which resulted in the revised edition, which included Siringo's opinions of the cowboy badman. Siringo's analysis in the revised edition of the causes of outlawry is reasonable.

According to one account, Siringo's first attempt at writing was a dime novel, "A Trip Up the Chisholm Trail; or Two Cowboys on the Buffalo Range," which was "quickly relegated to the bottom of a trunk."[14] A letter from Siringo to O. W. Nolen, written in June 1922, says that he had written another novel, "Prairie Flowers or Bronco Chiquita," "a novel about manhood and womanhood in the early days of Texas and the West," in which "the scene starts in Southwest Texas in 1845 and ends in Western Colorado in 1883, when the cow-girl heroine, Bronco Chiquita, married a Yankee and lived happily ever afterward."[15] No one has any information about the publication of the novel. Probably Siringo's last work of fiction, like his first, was buried in a trunk and was burned with the rest of his papers. When one considers the plot and the ambiguous gender of the heroine, he can be consoled by the thought that not much was lost. Siringo's forte was autobiography and bad men.

Most of the time the two areas were treated together. Siringo was the first cowboy autobiographer, the most prolific, and (I believe) the best. In order to examine his work thoroughly, we must look at the life of the man and at his environment. Too, we can understand the man only by looking at his autobiographical works.

CHAPTER 2

Beginnings: The Development
of the Cowboy

THE story of the early life of Charlie Siringo coincides with the development of the Range Cattle Industry in the southern part of Texas. Although no one would deny that cattle were raised in great numbers in states other than Texas and that small-scale cattle raisers took their cattle to market by driving them long before the time of trail driving from Texas to the Kansas markets, the fact still remains that in 1865 there were millions of longhorns in Webb's diamond-shaped area in South Texas and that by 1885 the Range Cattle Industry, characterized especially by the open range, had spread from South Texas to the Canadian border and from the western part of the Mississippi Valley to the Rocky Mountains.

This Range Cattle Industry, Webb's Cattle Kingdom, was made possible by the virtual wiping out of the large buffalo herds and by the subjugation of the Plains Indian tribes; by the existence of large areas of grasslands, virtually free for use if not for the taking; and by herds of relatively cheap cattle eager to harvest the grass.[1]

I   Where the Cowboy Came From

Charlie Siringo was ten years old when the Civil War ended. At an early age he became a cowboy and observed conditions which prevailed in the Gulf Coast country of Texas before trail driving began and before the Cattle Kingdom really developed. Three of his books, *A Texas Cow Boy*, *A Lone Star Cowboy*, and *Riata and Spurs*, describe in varying detail what happened in this early period.

When the Civil War ended, the longhorn cattle ranged mainly in the Coastal Plains and in the brush country, in an area bounded, roughly, by the Gulf of Mexico on the south and east, by the Rio Grande on the south and west, by the Indian frontier on the north and west (not far from San Antonio), and by settled farm country to the north and east of San Antonio. Both the South Plains and the Staked Plains (Llano Estacado) were the shooting grounds of the Plains Indians, who subsisted mainly on the great herds of buffalo.

But cattle ranged freely south of San Antonio; it was this area that the American cowboy came from; he was the occupational descendant of the Mexican *vaquero*, from whom he borrowed much in equipment, technique, and language ("lingo"). Exactly when the name "cowboy" began to be used has never been determined. According to J. Frank Dobie, the term was first used just after the establishment of the Republic of Texas in 1836, when Texan horsemen began to gather and appropriate cattle left by fleeing Mexicans. The riders, most of them young, were called "cowboys," perhaps in the same way that the word was applied to similar raiders during the American Revolution. Dobie says that the term was not then a respectable one; it still carries some of the odium originally attached to it.[2]

According to *The Papers of Mirabeau Buonaparte Lamar*, cited by Dobie, the contemporaries of those cowboys were intolerant of them, considering them blatant robbers: Lamar received bitter complaints about them. One well-organized crew, calling themselves the Band of Brothers, terrorized the area around Victoria, stealing from Anglo and Mexican alike. Other bands were called by irate Texans "cattle robbers" and "cow stealers." They were also highway robbers. The word "cowboy" gradually began to be applied to one gang of thieves, and then to all "cow drivers."[3]

The evolution of the term from its original meaning to the present glorified one has not been fully traced; perhaps it cannot be. The word did not appear in print generally until after the Civil War. Except as applied to the Tory guerrillas of the American Revolution, the earliest example of the use of the word in *A Dictionary of American English* is from a magazine article published in 1877.[4] John Young, in Dobie's *A Vaquero of the Brush Country*, states that in the early days the brush rider (and that describes most cowboys of the time) was called a *vaquero* or "hand" most of the time.[5] Siringo says that the term "cowboy" came into popular use during the first two years of the Civil War, when an attempt was made by boys not old enough to enlist in the army to hold the family cattle on the home range and keep the calves branded.

Because of their youth these riders were called "cowboys."[6]

Siringo realized that there was no such thing as a typical cowboy. Those who worked on ranches, even during the open-range period (which ended about 1885), were individuals. Siringo thought of himself as an individual; yet he also felt that he was representative of his group. In *Riata and Spurs* he writes, "In order to illustrate the environment of these young cowboys throughout the State of Texas from whence sprang the first cowboys, I will devote this chapter to my own young life and thoughts."[7]

Siringo thought that the daredevil cowboy was a product of the violence of the Civil War, of the presence of unlimited numbers of cattle in South Texas, most of them unbranded at the close of the war, and of the drives to Kansas. He accepted as fact the cowboy's tendency toward violence, saying that when boys of sixteen and eighteen were sent to the front to fight Yankees, they turned naturally toward gunpowder and the taking of lives. These same men, as veterans of the war, came into contact with the "robber-gambler" element in the tough cow towns of Kansas; the natural result was the gunfight. These men, Siringo believed, did not deserve their reputations; they were merely ready to defend their rights.[8] Siringo expressed dislike for a foreman who "gave him fits" for laying out a Negro "with a four year old club" and another time laid him out with his open hand for trying to carve one of the boys up with a butcher knife.[9]

Whether or not the carrying of weapons for self-defense was as common as the cliché-ridden Western story indicates is a matter of opinion. Control in the cow towns was sometimes exercised by the disarming of cowboys as they entered the towns. Most states passed antigun laws early, but in practice these laws seem to have been nullified by exceptions. The Texas law is typical; in 1871 the state legislature passed a law against carrying weapons, providing for a fine of from $25 to $100 for violations. The exceptions provided in the law, however, were so many that the law must have had a negligible effect. Exempt were law officers, a person on his own premises or in his place of business, persons traveling, and those fearing personal attack. Also exempt were those counties designated by the governor as frontier counties.[10] The statute seems to have had little immediate effect, although in the spring of 1876 Siringo was fined in Matagorda County for carrying a gun.[11] Ten years later he advised newcomers to the West to buy a pistol, "the most important ornament." He wrote,

If you are foolish enough to go without the latter [a pistol], the cooks at the different ranches where you happen to stop will not respect you. Instead of putting the handle to your family name, they will call you the sore-footed kid, old man Nibbs, or such names as these. We know from experience that the pistol carries much weight with it, and therefore especially advise the young "tenderfoot" to buy one, even if he has to ride barebacked. . . .[12]

Thus the times required that the cowboy carry a gun, even though the weapon was the source of much of his trouble. In an interview shortly before his death Siringo admitted that the cowboy did "lots of raw things." But his environment was raw; he was on the outskirts of civilization. Siringo believed, furthermore, that the violence of the cattleman's frontier was no worse than that of the East, where things were done "behind closed doors of polite society," evil acts committed frequently on impulse. Guns were universally worn in the West, he said, and this practice made the bad man seem worse than he was. Unless hindered by better judgment, the Westerner always had at hand the means to give "a mortal wound in exchange for an affront." Siringo also believed that the "fast draw," too fast for the eye to follow, was a fiction rather than a reality. Fiction writers exaggerated the gun fight; the real thing was bad enough.[13]

II   *The Making of a Cowboy*

It seems inevitable that Siringo should become a cowboy. He was born and lived his early years in the middle of cattle clatter. His birthplace, the "Dutch Settlement," was a small community on Matagorda Peninsula, which was a narrow strip of land varying in width from one to two miles, between the Gulf of Mexico and Matagorda Bay. The peninsula joins the mainland at the mouth of Caney Creek and extends in a general southwesterly direction along the coast for an estimated seventy-five miles, coming to a point at Decrow's Point. The "Dutch Settlement" lay about midway on the peninsula.[14]

The entire peninsula was unfenced as, indeed, was the surrounding area. Longhorn cattle covered the area, among them a small herd owned by Mrs. Siringo, who was a widow. This herd provided the Siringo family with meat and milk. Siringo learned to rope by practicing on the milk calves and holding them away from the cows while his mother did the milking. Because it took "about a dozen"

of the rangy longhorns to provide milk enough for the family,
Siringo had plenty of practice, both in roping and in riding the
calves; he became an expert, he says, "at a tender age."[15]

During the Civil War a Federal garrison was established at
Decrow's Point. In order to keep the Yankees from having free beef
to eat, some Texans rounded up "thousands" of longhorns on the
peninsula, including Mrs. Siringo's herd, drove them to the
mainland, and turned them loose with other cattle to "rustle for
themselves." There was only one cow left in the settlement—old
Browny, kept by Mrs. Siringo to provide milk for Charlie and his
sister to supplement their diet of "straight mush."

During the war the cattle turned loose on the mainland became
wild as deer, some of them ranging as far as two or three hundred
miles away, with all of the increase remaining unbranded. In the
spring of 1866 the young men of the peninsula and boys who were
old enough to ride went to the mainland, on Bay Prairie, on a
"cowhunt." They rounded up and returned to the peninsula about
a thousand longhorns, among them part of Mrs. Siringo's herd.
Charlie and his friend Billy Williams watched the hunt and longed
for the time when they would be cowboys, too.[16] In 1868, when
Mrs. Siringo married again and left Texas, she sold her cattle for a
dollar a head.[17]

Similar cowhunts were going on throughout the open-range section of South Texas. In 1866 and 1867, along the hundreds of miles
of coast, west to the Rio Grande and north to the Indian frontier,
many crews were organized to brand calves and mavericks which
had been left unbranded during the war. Siringo states that since
mavericks were then public property, legitimately belonging to
anyone who put his brand on them, mavericking became "all the
rage," the idea being to brand cattle while the supply lasted.[18]

Much folklore has developed around the origin of the word
"maverick," which meant an unbranded, unmarked, and unaltered
"cow brute." Siringo's explanation was a part of the folklore; it is
also typical of the free-wheeling style of A Texas Cow Boy:

> In early days, a man by the name of Mavrick settled on the Lavaca river
> and started a cow ranch. He being a chicken-hearted old rooster, wouldn't
> brand nor earmark any of his cattle. All his neighbors branded theirs,
> therefore Mr. Mavrick claimed everything that wore long ears.
>
> When the war broke out Mr. Mavrick had to bid adieu to wife and babies
> and go far away to fight for his country's good.

When the cruel war was ended, he went home and found his cattle roaming over a thousand hills. Everywhere he went he could see thousands and thousands of his long-eared cattle.

But when his neighbors and all the men in the surrounding country came home and went to branding their five years increase, Mr. Mavrick did not feel so rich. He made a terrible fuss about it, but it did no good, as in a very few years his cattle wore some enterprising man's brand and he was left out in the cold.

Hence the term "Mavrick." At first people used to say: "Yonder goes one of Mr. Mavrick's animals!" Now they say: "Yonder goes a Mavrick!"[19]

It is perhaps too bad that the account is not true; Siringo's story is more colorful than the truth. J. Frank Dobie gives the real history of the word. Samuel Maverick, who was not a rancher, but was a lawyer, in 1845 took four hundred cattle in on a debt, leaving them on Matagorda Island in the care of a Negro slave family, who did not brand the calves. He moved the slaves and the cattle to the mainland in 1853, but still only about a third of the calves were branded. Neighbors, surmising that at least some of the unbranded calves roaming the prairie were Maverick's, called them "mavericks" and "mavericked" them.[20]

Siringo's first job was as a mavericker, and he started young. From reading the reminiscences of old "stove-up" cowboys, one, if he is not careful, might picture the old-time cowboy as ancient. But it took young men to do the hard work of the range; some, like Siringo, began very young. He first worked for wages, ten dollars a month, for a Mr. Faldien in the spring of 1867, at the age of eleven. He had been envying the other boys, and when Faldien wanted to teach him to run cattle, Siringo "jumped at the chance" to become "a full-fledged cowboy, wearing broad sombrero, high-heeled boots, Mexican spurs, and the dignity of a full-grown man." The crew did nothing but hunt wild hogs and brand mavericks. Before his job was cut short by typhoid fever, Siringo wrote, he became handy with a rope because the mavericks had to be roped and thrown before they were branded.[21]

Siringo had found his calling. When his mother married and went north, Siringo and his sister went along. When his new stepfather turned out to be a drunkard, Siringo supported the family, working two years, mainly at St. Louis and at Lebanon, Illinois, as a farm laborer, a carpenter's helper, and a bellhop. He was sent to school several times by a New Orleans man named Myers, but once he had a knife fight with a schoolmate and another time a fight with the teacher. Myers wanted him to stay in school and make something out of himself, but Texas called. Siringo arrived in Indianola, Texas, in the fall of 1870, a stowaway on the Morgan liner, the *St. Mary*. He later remembered that he had shouted, when he stepped foot on Texas soil, "Back at last to the dear Lone Star State; the natural home of the cowboy and the longhorn steer."[22] Both were to be an important part of his life for many years.

III   *A Real "Cow Boy from Bitter Creek"*

Siringo did not, however, find immediate work as a cowboy; he went to work in a packing plant. In 1870, the third year of the trail drives to Kansas, the Gulf Coast area was still overstocked. Shipments made by coastal steamers had not been profitable. So slaughterhouses were established along the coast, as far south as the present site of Kingsville, most of them utilizing only the hides and tallow. One such slaughterhouse, five miles below Indianola, was operated by H. Selickson, and another was operated by W. B. Grimes on his Matagorda ranch. Grimes killed about two hundred cattle a day, most of them strays.

At various times, Siringo worked at both places, usually only until he could get a job on a ranch; on his arrival at Indianola he worked for Selickson for about two months. He spent his first month's wages for a fancy pistol and a part of the second month's pay for a pair of fancy star-topped boots. Typically, he lost the rest of his wages at "monte," a Mexican card game which was to be a trouble-maker for Siringo for much of his life.[23]

He went to work for Joseph Yeamans, a Baptist preacher who was trying to run a truck farm, but he did not like the job because Yeamans thought it was sinful to butcher a maverick for beef. Siringo did not approve of this breach of custom, insisting that it was the local practice never to eat one's own beef; the other man's tasted better. In fact, a hungry man seldom looked at the brand of the animal he killed for beef; cow brutes were plentiful.

At any rate, at the Yeamans farm Yeamans and his reluctant helper lived on black coffee, hard tack, and raccoon and opossum meat. Siringo, not able to stomach such fare with fat mavericks grazing all around, lasted only a month. He swore off farming and went to Matagorda, where, on about April 1, 1871, he hired out to

Tom Nye, a foreman of the Rancho Grande, where no scruples against eating another man's beef prevailed.[24]

Siringo remembered that once, somewhat later, "Shanghai" Pierce, one of the owners of the Rancho Grande, rode into a camp where Siringo and the other cowboys were butchering one of Pierce's beeves and remarked, "Boys, the day is coming when every man will have to eat his own beef."[25]

Pierce's Rancho Grande was one of the best-known ranches in the Gulf Coast country, and Abel H. ("Shanghai") Pierce was even better known. He was famous all over South Texas as a shrewd trader who managed to survive all of the economic maneuvers baffling even the other Yankees. He would ride into a cow camp on a fine horse, accompanied by a Negro who led a pack horse loaded with gold and silver. The money would be dumped on the ground until sale agreements were made with the cattlemen; then Pierce would empty the coins on a blanket and pay off in hard cash.

Pierce accumulated a large amount of land near Wharton and became one of the most famous of the trail drivers. His steers, raised in the Gulf Coast country, became known from the Rio Grande to the Canadian border as "Pierce's sea lions." He was famous for his size and for the piercing quality of his voice; no one who ever heard him sing or talk ever forgot him.[26]

At the time Siringo joined the Rancho Grande crew, the ranch was owned by Shanghai and his brother Jonathan, in partnership with Allen and Poole. "Old Shang," as Siringo called him, had come to Texas from Yankeeland before the Civil War, "poorer than skim milk," and had first worked for W. B. Grimes on Tres Palacios Creek, splitting live oak rails at a dollar a day. (Live oak is an especially hard, knotty wood.) By 1871 the Pierce brothers owned part interest in the Rancho Grande and over 100,000 longhorns. During the time when Siringo was working there, they sold out to Allen, Poole, and Company for $110,000. That shows, wrote Siringo, "what could be done in those days with no capital but lots of cheek and a branding iron."[27]

The difference between the Rancho Grande, a big operation, and the smaller ranches impressed sixteen-year-old Charlie greatly. The crew, consisting of Siringo and four other boys about his age, was taken by Tom Nye by sailboat from Matagorda to a line camp at Palacios Point, south of the present site of the town of Palacios. Other cowboys joined the group, which traveled overland to the

main headquarters at Deming's Bridge on Tres Palacios Creek,
branding mavericks and calves as they went. The main headquarters consisted of a bunkhouse and smaller buildings, a company
store, a residence for Jonathan Pierce, and a church building. There
were about fifty cowboys at the ranch, including a few Mexicans
and Negroes. The ranch was in a stir of activity in preparation for
spring work. Siringo's group arrived at headquarters just after Old
Shang had arrived from the Rio Grande Valley with a herd of three
hundred wild Mexican ponies. Pierce had bought them for $2.50 a
head because they were wet; that is, they were bought from Mexican rustlers, with the water of the Rio Grande still dripping from
their hides. Siringo describes this way of acquiring horses as a common one of the time.[28]

Siringo's first experience as a cowboy had been brief. Now he was
to become a full-fledged employee of a large ranch. His first action,
after arriving at ranch headquarters, was to head for the company
store, where he spent, on credit, three months' wages for an outfit
which made him look like a real "Cow Boy from Bitter Creek." He
bought a saddle, bridle, spurs, pistol, bowie knife, bedding, sombrero (hat), silk handkerchiefs, slicker (raincoat), and high-heeled
boots.[29] Like many other cowboys of the time, Siringo wore no belt,
because a tight belt sometimes caused hernia when the cowboy's
horse pitched. Many trusted to luck to keep their pants up; Siringo,
like the Mexican *vaquero*, wore a silk sash.[30]

Cowboy boots, still an important item of attire in the rural West,
were almost as important to Siringo as his saddle. He stated that the
cowboys took great pride in their small feet, often wearing boots
which were too small for them. When their boots were wet, they
were hard to get on and off; as a result a cowboy would often sleep
with his boots on. Once Siringo wore his boots night and day for
two weeks; they were number fives, when they should have been
sixes.[31]

In *A Texas Cow Boy* Siringo has much to say about the cowboy's
equipment. An outfit, he says, is somewhat like a Boston dude's
rig—it can be bought for a small or a large amount of money. A
fancy outfit would cost about $500: a saddle, $100; saddle blanket,
$50; quirt and riata, $25; pearl-handled Colt's .45, $50; Winchester
to match, $75; Angora goat leggings (chaps), $25; and a Spanish
pony, $25. His description resembles the account in "The Old
Chisholm Trail":

> On a ten dollar hoss and a forty-dollar saddle
> I'm goin' out West punchin' longhorn cattle.

On the other hand, Siringo wrote, a common serviceable outfit could be bought for $82: pony, $25; leggings, $5; saddle, $25; saddle blankets, $5; spurs, bridle, and stake rope, $5; and a Colt's .45, $12.[32]

Soon after he was equipped for work, Siringo, in a group of men bossed by Nye, was sent on a "cow hunt" in Lavaca and Jackson counties. Besides the crew there were two others, one working near the home ranch and the other on the Colorado River. Each crew consisted of about fifteen men. The remuda, or horse herd, of a crew consisted of a hundred Spanish ponies, most of them still wild. Some of the cowboys had trouble riding the wild horses, but Siringo was a good enough rider to stay on even when the pony pitched into the timber.

The life of the brush-country cowboy was not easy; the work was from "can to can't," the crew leaving camp before daybreak and coming back after dark. They tightened their belts (or silk sashes) instead of eating a noon meal, but two other meals made up for the deficiency. For breakfast they often ate pork and beans which had been simmering all night in a dutch oven over hot coals. Knives and forks were not used; the cowboys used their own pocket knives or bowie knives. At night the Negro cook had a hot meal, usually consisting of meat from a heifer calf, corn bread, molasses, and black coffee, waiting for them. Siringo particularly remembered meals of calf ribs broiled before the campfire and a large dutch oven full of loin, sweetbread, and heart, covered with flour gravy. The cowboys slept on the ground, having only a wagon sheet (tarpaulin) to turn the water when it rained.[33]

Most of the cattle gathered were old "mossy horns," some of them eighteen years old. Siringo says that although it is hard to believe, the steers had a fine coating of moss on their horns; the trees were covered with moss.[34] J. Frank Dobie says that the term "mossy horn" probably was based on the fact that many of the older steers had rough wrinkles on their horns and that their horns sometimes were twisted about with the low-hanging Spanish moss from the river bottom timber, where wild cattle took refuge.[35]

The gathering of these old mossy-horn steers was not easy. The cattle remained hidden in the heavy brush during the daytime, ven-

turing out on the small areas of prairie grass only at night. Consequently, the crew did most of their work in the early morning.
Siringo gives a description of a typical day.

About two hours before daylight the cook would yell "Chuck!"
and the boss would rouse the men out. After breakfast the horses,
which had been staked out during the night, were saddled, and the
whole crew would strike out for a predetermined clearing, a section
of the prairie land in the midst of the heavy brush. At the end of the
clearing they would dismount and wait for daylight.

The longhorns that had spent all their lives in the brush would, at
the first sight of a man on a horse, head for the nearest timber,
regardless of what was in the way. This was true, Siringo says, only
of the animal raised in the brush. The steers would graze in the
small clearings at night and at daylight would head for the brush,
grazing as they went. Then the cowboys would ride through the
brush until they reached the point towards which the steers were
heading. When it became good daylight, they would ride out
towards the herd, rope in hand.

The old mossy horns were usually on the alert, and as soon as one
of them saw the men, the entire herd would rush *toward* the cowboys. Then it was "catch as catch can." The cowboys would meet
the rushing herd, and each man would rope a steer, throw it, and tie
it down as quickly as he could, and then go to the rescue of anyone
else who might be having trouble. If a man roped a steer he could
not handle, he would have to do the best he could until someone
came to his aid.

Breaking in the steers so that they could be driven was a task in
itself. Often a steer that would not remain in the herd gave trouble.
Then the cowboys would sew up the steer's eyelids so that he could
not see to escape. That, says Siringo, would "bring him to his milk."

The work was not free of danger. Siringo, because he was a new
hand, got into several scrapes. Once, riding at full speed, he roped a
steer just at the edge of the timber. He could not stop his horse in
time to prevent the steer's going on one side of a tree and the horse
on the other. Because the rope was tied fast to the saddle horn,
Texas style, the steer, the horse, and the cowboy landed in a heap
against a tree. Another time, the same day, he roped a large steer,
which jerked his horse over backwards on him. When the horse got
up, Siringo was tangled in the rope, which still had an angry steer
on the other end trying its best to gore both horse and man. Siringo

hung on his horse, head down, until he was rescued by Jack, a Negro cowboy.[56]

The first herd Tom Nye put up was for a "short horn" named Black who had brought his crew of greenhorn Kansas boys overland from Wichita. By the time the herd was ready for delivery, Nye's crew was exhausted. Every steer had to be roped, thrown, and road-branded; all the cattle in a herd, no matter what the original brands were, carried the same road brand, which was burned into the hair (but not the hide) of the steers deep enough to last until the railhead was reached. It was hard even for the experienced cowboys to keep the steers together; on stormy nights every man was in the saddle all night, trying to avoid a stampede. Even Shanghai Pierce, who was a good horseman, would pierce the darkness with his famous voice in an effort to quiet the steers.

Finally, the herd was turned over to Black and his Kansas "short horn" cowboys, who started it for Kansas; many of them had never seen a Texas steer. Consequently, the crew crossed the Red River into the Indian Territory with nothing but the chuck wagon and the remuda, having lost every steer. Many of the steers returned to their home range, and Pierce had the pleasure of selling them again the next spring. Pierce later saw Black at Wichita, where, flat broke, he had gone back to his blacksmithing.[37]

IV   *Mavericking*

The foreman was one of the most important men on a ranch. The success of the enterprise depended largely on his ability and honesty. A ranch foreman who influenced Siringo greatly was Wiley Kuykendall, a brother-in-law of the Pierces. "Mr. Wiley" spent very little of his time in bed. He was living proof, Siringo says, that strong coffee and tobacco will not kill a man. He drank gallons of black coffee, steaming hot from the camp coffeepot; he got up with the cook, in order to get the first cup of hot coffee. Only when he was asleep did the smoke from his black pipe cease.

Each morning, when it was time to wake the crew, Kuykendall would walk to the area where the cowboys' beds were spread on the ground and say, "in a sweet, low, tender" voice, "Come, boys, come, get up and hear the little birds singing their sweet praises to God Almighty." Then his voice would become loud and angry: "Damn your souls, get up!"[38]

While working for Kuykendall, Siringo first became a cattle owner. Even as early as the seventies, ranchmen did not approve of their men owning cattle; later most cattlemen would not allow their men to run brands of their own. But while on a trip through Jackson County to brand mavericks for the company, Kuykendall decided that it would look more "businesslike" if he were to brand a few mavericks for himself. To keep the cowboys quiet, he gave each of them a "nest egg," that is, a few steers to "draw to." Siringo's nest egg, with the brand A T Connected (with the T above the A), consisted of a pair of two-year-olds. Naturally, after that Siringo carried a running iron (a short piece of iron curved at one end) tied to his saddle, so that he could brand a few mavericks for himself without Kuykendall's knowing about it. Frequently, when a likely looking maverick turned up, Siringo would capture the animal, build a small brush or cow-chip fire, and put his own brand on it. Allen and Poole got only the poorer ones. Everything ran along as smoothly "as if on greased wheels" for about two months, until Moore, the "big chief," heard of the mavericking and sent for the crew. Kuykendall, Siringo says, "got the G. B."—the good-bye—and another man took his place. (Siringo later, after reconsidering and in loyalty to Kuykendall, censored his language and the incident by writing, "Mr. Wiley severed his connection with the outfit.")[39]

Providing work for cowboys during the slack winter season was not nearly so great a problem as it later became on the colder North Plains. Since a general roundup in the brush country was impracticable, cow crews branded mavericks and calves continuously, in the winter as well as in the summer. Also, the Rancho Grande had other work for its men. Siringo spent one winter in the camp at Palacios Point, where a Morgan steamship landed twice a week to take on board cattle for the New Orleans market. Usually about five hundred steers were shipped each time. Often it would be midnight before the ship was loaded; then the cowboys would "have a picnic" at George Burkhart's store, where he kept plenty of "red-eye, the cowboy's delight." Often riderless ponies would arrive at the line camp, their riders having "fallen by the wayside."

While working on the Rancho Grande Siringo had an experience which, he believed, proved his toughness. While he was helping to drive a herd of steers to Richmond to be shipped by rail (the railroad was a small intrastate one), he had to take his clothes off to dry after he had helped swim the herd across a swollen stream. While he was standing barefooted in the tall grass, a rattlesnake bit him on the foot. "This," wrote Siringo, "caused the death of his snakeship, as I was angry and beat him to a pulp." His foot became so swollen that he could not wear his boot for a week, but he did not miss doing his full share of the work.[40]

A company store at ranch headquarters was very convenient for the men, but sometimes the disadvantages of the system outweighed the advantages.

Siringo, in December 1872, after having worked for the Rancho Grande for almost two years, quit and went to settle up at the company store. He had made extensive plans to spend the money he had coming. He had already picked out a dozen or so ponies which he knew were for sale; he was going to lead the easy life of a horse trader.

An old Irishman named "Hunky-dory" Brown kept the store. He did the settling up with the men. When Siringo walked in, Brown consulted his books and then laid $300 on the counter. After standing and eyeing the boy for a while, the old Irishman said,

"Allen, Poole, and Company owe you three hundred dollars." He paused. "And you owe Allen, Poole, and Company two hundred and ninety-nine dollars and a quarter."

Then he raked all but 75 cents back into the cash drawer. Since Siringo had freely taken advantage of the convenience of the company store and had kept no accounts of his purchases, all he could do was to take the "six-bits" and leave.[41]

V   At Loose Ends

It was not hard for a man on a horse to find work in South Texas in the 1870s. The three and a half years after Siringo quit the Rancho Grande were perhaps the most aimless years of his life. Among other things, he tried to become an independent businessman by running a sailboat, hauling freight, on Matagorda Bay; the drunken generosity of his partner soon put them out of business. He worked for W. B. Grimes for a while, skinning cattle and branding mavericks, and made a false start up the trail.

Even though the Chisholm Trail was becoming an avenue through which the ranges of South Texas were being thinned out, the Gulf Coast country was still overstocked. In cold weather many cattle would "get down" in the mud and freeze to death. Siringo saw as many as fifty dead cattle scattered over a small bedding ground. During the winter of 1872 - 1873, one of the worst years for

"die-ups," Siringo saw tens of thousands of dead cattle in the country around Matagorda Bay.[42]

Other old-timers, also, spoke of the great die-up of 1872 - 1873.
During that "skinning season" Jim Miller's outfit on the Nueces
River skinned 4,000 dead cattle. It was the custom of the country
that any man could take a "fallen hide," that is, a hide off a dead
cow, no matter what brand was on the hide. The ranchers of the
Gulf Coast area spoke of the skinning season much the same as they
spoke of the branding season. Some winters the settlers could count
on a good hide crop. The natural result of this custom was a new
type of theft. Instead of driving the cattle off the range, the thieves
merely killed them, took the hides, and left the carcass for the buz-
zards. When the ranchers, outraged because of having their cattle
killed, waged war on the thieves, what was called the Skinning War
developed.[43]

Siringo, also, killed cattle for their hides, although he claimed he
killed only old stray bulls that had drifted into the coastal area during the Civil War. While working for the Rancho Grande, Siringo
had helped to dehorn some of these old bulls, which Shanghai
Pierce had contracted to sell to the Cuban government. The contract was never fulfilled, and balls from Siringo's cap-and-ball Colt's
pistol made hides out of many of them. During the winter of the
great die-up, Siringo and Horace Yeamans, a boy about his own
age, went into partnership in the skinning business, branding
mavericks as a side line. Many cattle bogged down in Turtle Bayou,
near Horace Yeamans's home. Siringo claims that so many cattle
died in the bayou that a person could cross it by using the backs of
dead cattle as stepping stones.

Most of the boys' skinning was done, however, at Hamilton's
Point, where Palacios now stands. The hides were shipped to Indianola, and the first batch brought Siringo $114. The next ship-
ment was even more profitable. He, as did many other settlers, har-
vested a good hide crop.[44]

During the 1870s many cowboys in South Texas owned
"maverick brands" and, Siringo says, felt like cattle kings. The
catch was, however, that a mavericker who did not own land often
never saw the maverick after he branded it, because there were no
fences, and cattle grazed together over a large range area. So
maverickers like Siringo often sold their brands to ranchers with
large land holdings, who could look after several brands at once.

Siringo's first maverick brand was sold to George Hamilton in the spring of 1874 at $2 a head. Hamilton was to pay for the cattle as they were gathered during the coming seasons. The last payment was made to Siringo in 1879.

Siringo immediately registered a new brand in Matagorda County, this time selecting a stray brand, that is, one not on record in the county but carried by many cattle that had strayed in from farther north. He made W. B. Grimes pay him for several old steers—some of them as old as Siringo—which were butchered at Grimes's slaughter pen. During the next few years Siringo recorded several different brands; once he traded his interest in three brands to Horace Yeamans for fourteen dollars and a crippled pony.[45]

Mavericking and killing stray bulls made Siringo, as well as many other cowboys, unpopular with the cattlemen. Because of Siringo's activities a "certain wealthy cattleman" hired a "nigger killer" to waylay and kill him. Fortunately he escaped with only a bullet in the leg. He spent the next few months recovering from the wound, part of the time herding the children of the Pierce brothers to school. This, like Siringo's other tries at schooling, ended with a fight with the teacher.[46]

By the mid-1870s Siringo had become an excellent horseman. He even worked at a job that many cowboys would not tackle— breaking wild horses. He took a contract in late spring 1873 to break some wild horses at $2.50 per head. Some days he would ride as many as five wild horses, most of them vicious buckers. He worked alone; he says that a cowboy in those days thought it a disgrace to need help in saddling and riding a bronco. The horse was roped and thrown; then the hackamore and leather blinds were put on him. Then the horse was saddled; the blinds were removed, and the horse was allowed to buck around the corral. After the horse as exhausted, he was taken out of the corral and blinds put on again. Then the cowboy mounted and removed the blinds. Usually, Siringo says, it took about two hours to break a pony. After the horse was ridden about a dozen times, the last few times with a bit in his mouth, he was considered "broke."[47]

In 1876, at the age of twenty-one, Siringo was a "top hand," the product of the area "where the cowboy came from." He had helped round up mossy horns and knew what it took to handle them. Roping mavericks had made him an expert roper. Riding wild horses had improved his horsemanship. He was ready for the job that every young Texan in the 1860s and 1870s aspired to—a job with a crew taking a herd "up the trail."

CHAPTER 3

Up the Trail

ONE of the most dramatic occupations of the old-time cowboy was trail driving. It would be difficult to make a complete list of novels, good and bad, based on cattle drives to the North. It has been estimated that 34,000 men drove nearly 10 million cattle and 1 million stock horses up the trails to the North in about twenty-eight years of trail driving.[1]

Their experiences on the trail so impressed many of these men that during the first decades of this century they organized themselves into the Old-Time Trail Drivers Association; eventually, their descendants became members of the association. Sometime before 1920, George W. Saunders, president of the association, and J. Marvin Hunter, historian and editor, prevailed on hundreds of the old cowboys to write of their experiences on the trail. The first volume of *Trail Drivers of Texas* was published in 1920 and the second in 1923. A one-volume edition, which included everything in the original volumes, was published in 1925.[2] Also, almost a hundred book-length reminiscences of old-time cowboys have been published.[3] Many of them extol the glories and wonders of going up the trail.

Much of the cowboy's work was drudgery. Trail driving was hard, too, but it was made less onerous by a spirit of adventure that caused most of the ex-trail drivers to wish for the good old days when life was free and simple. Texans who were born too late to spend their summers looking at the south end of a northbound longhorn frequently were regretful. This in part explains the presence of the sons of the trail drivers in the Old-Time Trail Drivers Association. My father, born in 1879, often spoke of the trail drives. An uncle, whose father went up the trail many times, talked about the old days almost as if he, instead of his father, had been a trail driver.

Charlie Siringo's trips up the trail greatly influenced his life. He

36

in turn contributed much to the history of the Chisholm Trail and to the history of trail driving that is central to Texas and Southwestern literature. His books are important sources of trail driving lore. Few writers have described more fully life on the trail.

Trail driving did not begin with the opening of the Chisholm Trail, nor was the Chisholm Trail the only cattle trial to the North. The name, however, caught the imagination of the old-timers, and most of the trails to the North, at one time or another, have been called the Chisholm Trail.

I   *The Chisholm Trail*

The original Chisholm Trail was, in fact, merely a wagon trail laid out by Jesse Chisholm, a half-breed Indian trader. In 1867 few herds followed his wagon tracks into Abilene, Kansas, to Joseph G. McCoy's cattle pens, but beginning in 1868 and during the next several years, most of the herds followed Chisholm's track. Early in the 1870s the northern trail was almost universally called the Chisholm Trail.[4]

The trails to the north, because they provided a market for Texas cattle, made many rancher-businessmen wealthy. The ranges of South Texas had become overstocked during the Civil War. A market for these cattle was necessary to the development of the Range Cattle Industry, and the cattle trails provided this market.

In 1865 cattle—good longhorn steers—could be bought on the Texas ranges for $3 and $4 a head. The same cattle in the markets of the north would have brought $30 or $40.[5] There was a great profit to be made, a veritable windfall,[6] but the cattle had to be transported to the Northern markets. The cattle trails and the long legs of the longhorns provided the transportation.

In 1915 Siringo became interested in the history of the Chisholm Trail and set out not only to mark the route of the trail but to determine its origin. Siringo's markers were to consist of large pairs of aluminum steer horns mounted on lengths of galvanized pipe set in concrete. He had already contracted with a firm in Erie, Pennsylvania, to furnish the horns when World War I caused the price of aluminum to rise. The contract was never completed.[7]

At the same time he had begun to correspond with several ex-trail drivers about the origin of the trail. His version of the history of the trail, his chief information coming from David M. Sutherland, was given in the revised *Riata and Spurs*. His dates seem to be inaccurate, but even (especially?) the members of the Old-Time Trail

Drivers Association were not in agreement as to dates, the origin, and the route of the trail.

Siringo writes that in 1867 the United States government decided to move the more than 3,000 Indians of the Wichita and affiliated tribes to a new reservation in the southern part of the Indian Territory. Previously (Siringo does not say when), Major Henry Shanklin, who was in charge of the Indians, paid Jesse Chisholm, "a rich half-breed squawman," to open a trail and establish supply depots along the trail through the Indian Territory to the Red River, the border between Texas and the Indian Territory. With a large ox train Chisholm went to Fort Leavenworth, Kansas, to load up with government supplies. Then he drove a hundred wild ponies through the Territory, to settle the quicksand in the Salt Fork, the Cimarron, the North Canadian, and the South Canadian rivers. After the trail was laid out, the 3,000 Indians, with their thousands of ponies and their soldier escort, traveled over it, making a plain roadway across the Indian Territory. This roadway was later called the Chisholm Trail. Millions of longhorns passed over the trail during the following years. Siringo was especially eager to clear up the confusion between Jesse Chisholm and Jinglebob John Chisum, a New Mexico rancher who had nothing to do with the Chisholm trail and whose only connection with Jesse was that their names were pronounced alike. Some historians have not yet realized this difference.[8]

In 1866 drives were made to Missouri, the route crossing the southeast corner of Kansas, near Baxter Springs, into Missouri. Siringo's old friend Wiley Kuykendall made one such trip.[9] In 1867, Siringo says, other herds headed north, their destinations uncertain. Some went to Wichita, Kansas, and a few to Abilene, which later became an important shipping center. In 1871, the Union Pacific hired David M. Sutherland, Siringo's chief source, and Major Shanklin, mentioned above, to turn herds from the Baxter Springs route into the Chisholm Trail to Abilene. In April 1871 Sutherland marked a cut-off trail with plows from Pilot Point to Bolivar, Texas. From Bolivar to Red River Station there was a plain wagon trail.[10]

Siringo's account of the origin of the Trail seems accurate, with the possible exception of the dates. His information came from a man closely associated with Major Shanklin, who supervised the removal of the Indians. It has been established that Major Shanklin was in charge of such an Indian removal in 1867. Martha Buntin writes that on September 29, 1866, a contract was let to Charles B. Johnson of Sherman, Texas, to remove the Indians from Kansas to the agency in the southern part of the Indian Territory. Chisholm's ranch was the starting place. The Indians arrived at their destination on November 18, 1867. Rupert N. Richardson writes that Henry Shanklin was in charge of a group of Wichitas and allied tribes in Southwestern Indian Territory in April 1868, having moved there from an area near Wichita previously. Sam Ridings, however, gives the time of the removal as 1868.[11]

Siringo gives the impression that there was little movement of cattle up the trail before 1870. His information is not completely accurate, although other ex-trail drivers also report that few herds went up the Chisholm Trail until 1870. George W. Saunders states that a few of the most venturesome cattlemen took herds to New Orleans, Baxter Springs, Abilene, and other markets in 1867 and 1868. More tackled the trail in 1869, and by 1870 trail driving was "all the rage."[12]

The route of the Chisholm Trail has been the subject of considerable controversy among those who went up the trail. The actual routes and branches of the trails have been charted elsewhere.[13] The cowboys, as they were driving cattle north, cared little about trail names. Ridings says that the Chisholm Trail ran from San Antonio to Abilene. Siringo states that the "Chisholm Trail proper" began at Austin.[14]

Actually, as can be seen from Wayne Gard's maps, all trails leading to the main trail were called the Chisholm Trail, even the Western Trail to Dodge City, which, because of the encroachment of the "fool hoe men" was moved westward.[15]

II   *Listen to My Tale*

Siringo's first trip to Kansas was on the Eastern Route, the Chisholm Trail proper; later, he went up the Western Trail to Dodge City. On about April 1, 1876, he took a job with W. B. Grimes, at $30 per month, to help drive a herd to Kansas. Siringo was past twenty-one years old, older than many of the cowboys who made the drive. He was of medium height—perhaps short—and slight of build, but ten years of experience on the ranges of South Texas had made him wiry and tough. His size and general appearance caused people to think him much younger than he actually was. Four years later, aged twenty-five, he still looked like a "smooth-faced kid."[16]

Siringo had started up the trail two years before, working with a crew of Kansas "shorthorns" (tenderfeet), but, after several stampedes, he quit because the boss, Jim Muckleroy, wanted him to break wild horses for the shorthorns, in addition to his regular duties, at no extra pay.[17] It might be noted here that the likening of the trail drive to an ocean voyage, where one signs on for the duration and cannot quit, is the product of the imagination of the fiction writer. Siringo quit when he got ready to, as did many others.

The Grimes herd which Siringo helped drive up the trail in 1876 was probably similar to many herds of the time. Few large herds, again despite accounts in pulp Westerns, ever existed. This herd was made up of 2,500 big mossy-horn steers gathered on the Navidad and Guadalupe rivers in Colorado, Jackson, and Victoria counties in the same way Siringo had helped round them up on the Rancho Grande several years before. The crew at first consisted of the boss, Asa Dowdy, twenty-five cowboys, and a cook. Later, at Austin, half the crew turned back, leaving twelve cowboys, each of whom had six picked Spanish ponies, the best available, in his mount. Grimes's road brand—a large G—was burned lightly into the hair of each steer, sufficiently deep to last until the trail drive was completed. Because the hide was not seared, the brand was only temporary.[18]

The life of the trail hand (Siringo did not use the term "drover") was not easy, but evidently the adventure, or at least the travel, attracted many young men. The cowboy was on duty twenty-five hours a day, always ready for trouble of any kind, especially stampedes. At best he worked all day and then spent part of the night watching the herd. If a herd stampeded often, he spent both his days and his nights in the saddle. Crossing swollen rivers, trying to stop stampedes, and trying to outwit harassing Indians were all a part of his routine. It was hard for him to keep clean; most of the time he slept in his clothes. And there was always the danger of injury or even death.

III   Stampede!

It was unusual for a herd of wild longhorns to make the long walk to Kansas without stampeding at least once. Stampedes frequently occurred during the first days of a drive, before the herd was trail broken. The Grimes herd was probably typical; it stampeded often. It was touchy; even the striking of a match or a horse's shaking its saddle would cause a run. Because the drive began in the spring, the season for thunderstorms in South Texas, the cowboys got little sleep. They stayed in the saddle all night watching the restless herd.

Consequently, when the herd reached Gonzales, Dowdy wanted to give the men a good night's rest. He did, according to Siringo, a very foolish thing. He put the herd up in a pen. A few miles west of town, on the House Ranch, there was a large public corral, built of large live oak logs and rails, with the largest logs on the bottom, next to the ground. The corral was round, so that if the herd stampeded, the cowboys, by yelling and flapping their slickers, could cause the cattle to mill until they were exhausted. The herd was driven into the corral, which was "jammed full."

After supper, the cowboys took the bedding and night horses to the corral and spread their beds around it, equal distances apart. There they bedded down, with their clothes on, holding the bridle reins or the hackamore ropes of their ponies.

After midnight, when the men were sleeping soundly, a thunderstorm moved in. With the first flash of lightning and the accompanying loud crash of thunder, the frightened herd stampeded, crashing through the fence near where Siringo slept. The fence disintegrated as though it were made of paper. Siringo barely had time to mount his pony and ride ahead of the herd. Looking back when the lightning flashed, he could see that the cattle were so tightly jammed together that fence rails were still riding on their backs.

Meanwhile, back at the camp, Dowdy had slept more comfortably, with his boots and outer clothing removed, his night horse tied to a wagon wheel. When the herd stampeded, he mounted his horse and soon reached the lead, riding barefooted, dressed only in his underwear. During the run his pony banged into a tree, tearing one of Dowdy's toes almost off.

The herd, as it reached the prairie about a mile from camp, split. Dowdy and Siringo stayed with one bunch. At dawn, after the steers had exhausted themselves, Siringo and Dowdy found themselves about ten miles from camp. Dowdy was in great pain. His toe was dangling, held only by the larger cords. Siringo put the toe back in place and tied it up in a handkerchief. As the two men drove the steers back to camp, following the muddy trail of the night before, they saw many steers with broken legs and knocked-down horns, the result of collision with the corral fence or with trees.[19]

IV   *Fool Hoe Men*

In 1876 Siringo observed conditions which later caused the trail to be moved farther west. The crew of the Grimes herd had several brushes with settlers near the trail. At Fort Worth Siringo saw a rapidly growing town, stirring because of the construction of the Texas and Pacific, Fort Worth's first railroad. The Grimes herd was driven through the east end of town, an area covered with unpainted frame shanties. Dogs rushed out from under the houses, barking at the steers. The resulting stampede expedited the herd's passage through the town, and the occupants of the new shanties became greatly excited at the sight.

North of Fort Worth the trail drivers found many of the watering places fenced off by settlers with the new barbed wire. The cowboys paid no attention to the fences but watered the cattle as usual. During one stampede, barbed wire hung to the horns and tails of the cattle. Siringo writes,

. . . the big and little "hoe men" ran out to sick the dogs on us. Some of these dogs "bit the dust" by having hot lead shot into them by angry cowboys, who regarded the "Chisholm Trail" too sacred to be scratched with plows and hoes.[20]

V   *River Crossings and Indian Scares*

When the herd reached the Red River, it was a raging torrent, nearly a mile wide. Unable to cross, about twenty trail herds were positioned along the river. The cowboys, Siringo wrote, would get together at night and talk and sing "mostly old favorites, such as Sam Bass, Mustang Grey, The Dying Cowboy, and When You and I Were Young Maggie."[21] The second evening a cattle inspector from Red River Station visited all the camps. He told the trail bosses that he would begin inspecting the herds early the next morning. This inspector, an employee of the State of Texas, was unpopular for two reasons: he charged a fee of ten cents a head for inspecting the cattle, and he checked the road brands and cut out all the range cattle that had "wandered" into the trail herds. So the trail drivers, a "Wess Harding bunch of cowboys," decided to "fix" the inspector.

At daylight the next morning, when the inspector rode into the nearest camp to begin his inspection, the cowboys were eating breakfast. The trail boss, an advocate of good old Texas hospitality, invited him to get down and have a cup of coffee. Then the cowboys threw him to the ground and "hog tied" him, gagging him with a handkerchief. Next they clipped the tail and mane of his fine Kentucky mare, cut into the hair on her side the message "the inspector is fixed," and turned her loose to go home. The news of the inspector's status was relayed to the other herds.

Dowdy, when he heard the news, immediately drove his herd across the river, saving not only the inspection fee of about $250 but the strays also. In the hurry of pushing the herd across the Red River an incident occurred which Siringo claimed left a blotch on his conscience. The yelling of the cowboys brought about a hundred fine, pureblood Durham cattle out of the brush; Siringo, watching them "in open-mouth wonder," let them enter the trail herd. The cattle, evidently the property of a local settler, were sold in Wichita for "big money." Possibly the blotch was caused by the fact that the money went into Daddy Grimes's pocket, not Siringo's. Later Siringo found out that after two days the inspector was located in the plum thicket where the cowboys had hid him. After he recovered, he sold out and moved to Kentucky.[22]

Siringo's accounts of trail driving include all of the hardships and incidents which are the basis of the many reminiscences by other old-time trail drivers. Unlike most of the brief accounts in *The Trail Drivers of Texas*, which Teddy Blue Abbott said seemed to have been written by a bunch of preachers,[23] there was life in Siringo's descriptions. He was able to see some humor in nearly everything that happened. An example is his account of the trail drivers' first Indian scare:

Everything went on lovely with the exception of swimming swollen streams, fighting now and then among ourselves and a stampede every stormy night, until we arrived on the Canadian river in the Indian territory; there we had a little indian [sic] scare. When within a few minutes of the river, Dawdy [sic] went on ahead to look up a good crossing; it wasn't long until we discovered a terrible dust coming, but instead of that it was our boss returning. He galloped up almost out of wind, telling us to stop the herd and make preparations for war, as the woods along the river were covered with indians [sic] on the war path.

After getting everything in shape for war, he selected two of his best armed men, which happened to be Otto Draub and myself, to go back with him and make peace with the red devils. We scoured the woods out thoroughly, but only succeeded in finding one old, blind "buck." Asa had, no doubt seen him and imagined the rest.[24]

Later on, Siringo saw many more Indians, who, he says, practiced

a sort of blackmail on most trail herds. They would ride into camp
when the cook was alone, eat everything in sight, and then demand
"whoa-haws" (steers). If they were not given beef, they would
stampede the herd at night.[25]

Swollen rivers in the Indian Territory gave trail herds much trouble. The Washita and the Canadian rivers were especially bad.
Again, Siringo's accounts of his first trail drive give the most detailed descriptions of crossing rivers which were "on the rise" that I
have seen. One incident on the first trail drive will illustrate the trail
drivers' troubles with river crossings.

The river was the Salt Fork, near the Kansas line. It was raining
hard when the herd reached the Salt Fork. Dowdy went ahead of
the herd to get the chuck wagon and the extra wagon (for water and
wood) across the river. The wagons had just reached the north bank
of the river, when trees and driftwood began coming down the
stream. Dowdy galloped back to the herd, shouting, "Whoop 'em
up, boys! She's rising a foot every second!"

When the herd reached the river, it was bank full, about a half-
mile wide, full of driftwood, and still rising. The chuck wagon was
on the other side of the river. The cowboys headed the lead steers
into the foaming river, and the herd followed, Henry Coats was in
the lead, Dowdy and Otto Draub were on the left point, and a
Negro cowboy, Gabe, and Siringo were on the right point.

The steers were following Coats nicely until he reached deep
water. His horse refused to swim, fell over on its side, and went under. The steers then turned on Gabe and Siringo and headed back
to the bank. Coats nearly drowned. Several efforts were made to get
the herd back into the water, but it was too late. The river continued to rise until it was about a mile wide. Siringo thought that
the refusal of the herd to "take the water" was a godsend, because
often cowboys drowned trying to make such a crossing. But the
crew was "in a fix," with the swollen river separating them from
their "grub" and bedding.

The herd was driven down the river a mile or two to timber.
There a fire was built, large enough not to be put out by the driving
rain. A large steer was butchered, and each cowboy roasted his supper over the fire, eating it without salt. Siringo's only variation from
this diet during the next seven days was part of an ear of corn which
he and Gabe found beside the trail. The two men sneaked away and
roasted and ate the corn, Gabe contending and Siringo agreeing
that God had dropped the corn there for their special benefit. The

days and nights were spent closely guarding the steers, since thunderstorms caused frequent stampedes. The Cimarron and Wild Horse rivers, south of the herd, were also raging. Consequently, the Grimes herd was isolated.

On the seventh day Siringo, Dowdy, and a man named Hastings were hunting steers near the Wild Horse, when they saw the tents of a company of United States soldiers across the "wicked little stream." The army captain told them they could have all the food they wanted if they would come after it. Dowdy and Hastings looked at Siringo, who was considered a good swimmer, as if to say that it all depended on him. Siringo shed his heaviest clothing (there were officers' wives in the camp) and jumped his pony, Yankee Doodle, into the water. The captain, after finding that the cowboys had been without food other than beef, ordered the cook to bring out some cold biscuits. After Siringo "got his fists full," the rest were thrown one by one across a narrow part of the stream to the other men. After he had eaten several biscuits, Siringo borrowed a washtub from the captain's wife, filled it with food, and floated it across to the other side. He then brought the tub back to the captain's wife, thanked her, and swam his horse back across, "feeling a thousand per cent better." That night the cowboys feasted, baking bread over the fire on sticks, and drinking coffee out of tin cans.

The next morning the sun came out. The river had gone down so that the herd, when it crossed that afternoon, had to swim only about a hundred yards. The cook and the driver of the wood wagon were found well-rested at a ranch on Pond Creek near the Kansas line. The herd entered Kansas near Caldwell, and Dowdy established a permanent camp on Ninnescah River, on July 4, 1876. Siringo probably rode his horse Yankee Doodle that day.[26]

VI   *End of the Trail*

The trail drivers' job was completed when the herds arrived at the Kansas cow towns. Sometimes the cowboys found it hard to decide what to do, after the customary spree. Those who wanted to return to Texas were given a ticket home. Others stayed with the herds until they were sold or drove them farther north. A few, like John Marcum of Siringo's crew, homesteaded in Kansas. When the herd reached the Ninnescah River, the owner, W. B. Grimes, who had come to Kansas by train, was there to meet it. He paid some of the cowboys off and bought their tickets home, but Siringo decided

to remain with a part of the herd, which had been split up to be fat-
tened for market.

The crew with which Siringo worked was similar to those which
he later bossed on the High Plains. In it were four riders, including
the boss, with five horses to the rider, and the cook, who drove the
chuck wagon. Two men would herd the cattle until noon, and the
other two would herd them until bedding-down time. The nights
were divided into four shifts, with one man on duty, unless there
was a storm.[27]

Siringo describes his off-duty activities vividly in a paragraph
which typifies his style:

I spent all my extra time when not on duty, visiting a couple of New York
damsels, who lived with their parents five miles east of our camp. They
were the only young ladies in the neighborhood, the country being very
thinly settled then, therefore the boys thought I was very "cheeky"—
getting on courting terms with them so quick. One of them finally "put a
head on me"—or in grammatical words, give me a black eye—which chop-
ped my visits short off; she didn't understand the Texas way of proposing
for one's hand in marriage, was what caused the fracas. She was cleaning
roasting-ears for dinner when I asked her how she would like to jump into
double harness and trot through life with me? The air was full of flying
roasting-ears for a few seconds—one of them striking me over the left eye—
and shortly afterwards a young Cow Puncher rode into the camp with one
eye in a sling. You can imagine the boys giving it to me about monkeying
with civilized girls, etc.[28]

The same New York family furnished the cowboys with eggs and
vegetables. Watermelons and cantaloupes did not cost them
anything; all they had to do was to load the chuck wagon with dry
cow chips from an old bedding ground, dump them out at the
kitchen door, and then load the wagon with melons. The settlers
burned the cow chips, hardened manure, sometimes called "prairie
coal," for fuel.[29]

A phenomenon almost universally described by the old-time cowboy writer was the end-of-the-trail celebration at the Kansas cow-
town, where the Texas cowboy gained his reputation for being
rough and tough. The cowboys' town activities can perhaps be compared to the shore leave of sailors who have seen extensive sea duty.
Siringo believed that the rough elements in the Northern cow towns
helped to turn the cowboy bad man in the wrong direction. Good-
natured celebrations often ended in tragedy.

In an interview shortly before his death Siringo talked of the cowboy's tendency toward violence, expressing ideas which his books reveal that he had held all his life. He stated that while the cowboy did lots of "raw things," he lived in the "rawest" surroundings. He believed that as many impulsive acts, fully as bad as the cowboys' deeds, were committed in supposedly polite society in the twentieth century, the difference being the cowboys committed their deeds in a free, open style. Siringo believed that the universal practice of wearing guns made the cowboy bad men seem really bad; they always had at hand a tool with which to give a mortal wound in exchange for an affront, unless better judgment prevailed.[30]

On about August 1, 1876, Siringo and another cowboy had an opportunity to go to Wichita, then a lively town of about 2,500. He and the other cowboy rode the thirty-five miles to town in "quick time." The first thing they did, Siringo states, was to go to the "New York store" and "fit out" with new clothes from head to foot. By the time the barbers finished fixing them up, it was dark. In the meantime Siringo and his friend had paid visits to various saloons, not merely as sightseers, and they were feeling gay. They mounted their horses and struck out in a gallop for Rowdy Joe's dance hall across the Arkansas River. Rowdy Joe's had the reputation among South Texas cowboys of being the "swiftest joint" in Kansas.

As the cowboys neared the toll bridge, the one-legged keeper came out of his shanty to collect the 25-cent toll. The riders passed him on the run, firing their pistols over his head. When they were halfway across the bridge, the toll collector "turned both barrels of a shot gun" loose at them. They could hear the buckshot rolling along the bridge floor at the horses' feet. One buckshot lodged in the calf of Siringo's left leg, the scar remaining, he says, to remind him of Wichita's "hurrah days."[31]

VII *The Trail Home*

Sometimes cowboys were, for various reasons, without a job in one of the Northern towns when winter came. Siringo was one of them in 1876. Late in the fall he "pulled up stakes" and left the Grimes herd. Although he seemed to have forgotten his reason for leaving when he wrote the later books, he gave the reason in *A Texas Cow Boy*. His best girl friend in Texas, thinking he had forgotten her, had married Siringo's friend, Billy Williams. When he received the letter bearing the bad news, Siringo, considerably wrought up, decided to go to the Black Hills, scene of a recent gold rush, where, he was sure, somebody would kill him. He and another cowboy, Collier, went to Wichita and settled up with Daddy Grimes, then proceeded to "whoop her up Liza Jane"—to take in the town of Wichita. At the end of two or three days of carousing they were "busted."

Not having enough money to take them to the Black Hills, the scene of Siringo's anticipated death, the cowboys headed toward the Medicine River, a hundred miles west, to hunt a winter job. Collier found a job at Kiowa, on the Medicine. Siringo drifted aimlessly southwest. The first night he slept out in the brush. The next day he took the first job offered him, one which would last only a month.

For $25 dollars a month (and board) and feed for Whiskey Pete, his horse, Siringo helped drive Gus Johnson's herd from his camp at the forks of Driftwood and Little Mule creeks south into the Indian Territory, where the herd was to graze all winter. Then, without a job, Siringo decided to do some trapping. He bought enough provisions to last him through the winter and built a house out of dry poles covered with grass, with a sod chimney. The first day the fireplace set the house afire, and he lost some of his food. Then he built a dugout in the bank of a stream, covering it over with poles and sod. Although the weather was cold, the dugout was fairly comfortable. However, the convenient dugouts, easily built by digging back into the bank of a stream or an arroyo so that only a roof and front need be constructed, were not always safe, especially in cattle country. One morning Siringo crawled out of the dugout to feed his horse and found himself in a blizzard. After making Whiskey Pete comfortable, he crawled back into his hole; he writes,

It was three or four o'clock in the evening, while humped up before a blazing fire, thinking of days gone by, that all at once, before I had time to think, a large red steer came tumbling down head first, just missing me by a few inches. In traveling ahead of the storm the whole Johnson herd had passed right over me, but luckily only one broke through.

Talk about your ticklish places! That was truly one of them; a steer jammed in between me and daylight and a hot fire roasting me by inches.

I tried to get up through the roof—it being only a foot above my head—but failed. Finally the old steer made a terrible struggle, just about the time I was fixing to turn my wicked soul over to the Lord, and I got a glimpse of daylight under his flanks. I made a dive for it and by tight squeezing I saved my life.

After getting out and shaking myself I made a vow that I wold leave that God-forsaken country in less than twenty-four hours, and I did so.[32]

But trouble usually follows trouble. Discarding his pelts, Siringo traveled southeast down Eagle Chief Creek and the Cimarron River. The third day the grass around his camp caught fire, burning up all his equipment except the clothing he wore, his saddle, and his saddle blanket. He continued south to Erin Spring, finally arriving in Paul's Valley, where he spent the entire winter breaking horses at $2.50 a head. He won considerable money racing Whiskey Pete, was "locoed" by a pretty half-breed Indian girl, and had a "wild time" in general, coming out of winter carrying two bullet wounds.[33]

VIII *Up the Trail Again*

Many cowboys rode up the trail only once, and many made the trip several times, quitting only when the trail drives ended in the 1880s. Early in the spring of 1877 Siringo drifted to Denison, Texas, and west to Gainesville and then to Saint Jo, on the Chisholm Trail. There he took a job with a herd owned by George W. Littlefield, cattle king of Austin, Texas, and bossed by Jim Wells. Having described life on the trail once, Siringo does not go into detail about the second trip. He merely states that the crew suffered many hardships in the Indian Territory, especially in crossing swollen streams. Once Siringo, surrounded by milling cattle in mid-stream, had to crawl to safety over the backs of cattle. At the Cimarron River at the mouth of Turkey Creek, the herd was turned northwest toward Dodge City, which was later the main terminus of the Western Trail. Even then, Siringo states, the "fool hoe-men" were rapidly settling up the country west of Wichita, making it hard to drive herds through. The Littlefield herd was driven to Nebraska and possibly into Montana. But when it reached Dodge City Siringo drew his pay and set out to celebrate Independence Day.

Siringo says that Dodge City was the "toughest cattle town on earth." The Atchison, Topeka and Santa Fe railroad was building west from Dodge City in 1877, and the usual hangers-on ("cutthroats and bums," Siringo calls them) filled the town. Dodge was also the supplies center for crews of buffalo hunters who were slaughtering the buffalo in the area surrounding Dodge, some of them traveling hundreds of miles away. In addition, in 1877 Dodge

City became the "long-horn cattle center of the Universe." Wichita
and Abilene had lost most of the herds because of settlers in Kansas
and Texas closing off the trails and fencing the water holes. On July
4, 1877, Siringo says, there were already eighty-one graves in Dodge
City's "Boot Hill" cemetery.

Siringo's celebration indirectly caused him to accept the job
which he held until 1883. On the night of July 4 he met his old
friend Wess Adams, and the two went on a drunken spree. They entered the Lone Star Dance Hall, then operated by the famous Bat
Masterson. The hall was filled with "free-and-easy girls, long-haired
buffalo hunters and wild and wooly [sic] cowboys." Adams started a
fight with a long-haired buffalo hunter to show the superiority of
"the cowboy class," and, when the hunter stabbed Adams in the
back, Siringo helped the wounded man out of the hall and to their
horses, which were hitched nearby. After they had mounted, Joe
Mason, a town marshal, tried to arrest them, but they drove him to
cover in an alley and left town in a hurry, firing their pistols into the
air. They rode to David T. Beals's camp, where Adams was laid up
for two weeks because of the loss of blood.[34]

Siringo's comment on the incident reveals his attitude toward the
violence of the cow town:

This incident illustrates what fools some young cowboys were after long
drives "up the Chisholm trail," and after filling their hides full of the
poison liquors manufactured to put the red-shirted Irish rail-road builders
to sleep, so that the toughs could "roll" them, and get their "wads." Instead of putting a cowboy to sleep it stirred up the devil in his make-up,
and made him a wide-awake hyena.[35]

IX   *To the Panhandle*

While Adams was recovering, Siringo went to work for the David
T. Beals Company to drive a herd of young steers to the Texas Panhandle, where a new ranch was being established. The new job was
a turning point for him. The Range Cattle Industry was moving into
the High Plains of Texas, and Siringo was a part of that movement,
a cowboy on one of the early ranches established there.

CHAPTER 4

To the High Plains

THE cattle trails to the North led to a profitable market for Texas beef. Extended, they also led to new areas so that the cattle industry of the open range, as it existed in South Texas, spread throughout the Northern Great Plains, especially to Kansas, Colorado, Nebraska, the Dakotas, Wyoming, and Montana. Siringo did not, as did many other cowboys, follow the herds to Nebraska, Wyoming, and Montana, where Texas cowboys helped to develop a cattle-raising system. He remained in Texas where, with the subjugation of the Indians, the Range Cattle Industry was rapidly spreading to Northwest Texas, especially to what is now called the Texas Panhandle. This is basically flat country—true plains, with little timber and an average annual rainfall of less than twenty inches. It is high country; the altitude of present-day Lubbock is more than 3,000 feet, and sections of Dallam County, at the northwest corner of the Panhandle, are 4,600 feet above sea level.[1]

I Indians and Buffalo

The spread of the Cattle Kingdom to the High Plains of Texas was similar to its spread to the Northern Plains states. Therefore, what happened in Texas was typical of developments throughout the Great Plains area.

During the first few years of the trail drives, in the period immediately after the Civil War, there were no ranches on the High Plains. The grasslands of the Texas Panhandle were the range of the buffalo and the Plains Indian, whose free existence depended on the buffalo. Cattlemen had long known that land which would support the huge buffalo herds would also support herds of longhorns—but not at the same time. Therefore the barrier to the dominance of the High Plains by the Range Cattle Industry was the presence of the

51

buffalo and the Indians. The two cultures, cattleman and Indian, could not freely exist in the same geographical area.

In the late 1860s the Comanches, the bane of Texan pioneer existence, raided Texas settlements frequently, despite efforts of the Indian Service and the United States Army to keep them on reservations. The Indian Service vacillated between humanitarian and rigidly authoritarian policies. So long as the Indians had horses and weapons and herds of buffalo to hunt, the Army had no way of controlling them.

Beginning in 1871, General Mackenzie led several campaigns against the Comanches. The end of Comanche dominance of the High Plains was marked by Mackenzie's trapping of the Indians in the Palo Duro Canyon and the killing of their horses. By 1875 Indian raids in the High Plains had virtually ceased. Buffalo herds were being killed off, the policy of the Indian Service was stronger, and Texas had developed a strong force of Texas Rangers.[2] Fort Elliot was established in the eastern part of the Panhandle, in what is now Wheeler County, and Indians were forbidden to enter the region. Soon reasonable safety for settlement was assured.[3]

II   Short Grass and Longhorns

Ranchers began to drive cattle into the Panhandle and to establish ranches. All that was necessary was to drive a herd of longhorns into the free range of the Panhandle and to find water for them. The herd would graze slowly into the grassy area while the owner rode ahead and located a ranch headquarters, usually near a stream. The building of a temporary headquarters building, usually a dugout, established the ranch.

In 1876 the first herd, that of Charles Goodnight, entered the Texas Panhandle from New Mexico. Goodnight had started towards Texas from Colorado in 1875, but rumors of Indian raids had turned him aside into New Mexico. In the spring of 1876 the cattle were driven slowly down the Canadian River to Tascosa, northwest of present-day Amarillo, then south to the Palo Duro Canyon, east of present-day Canyon, a range which Goodnight had chosen when he was a Texas Ranger. The Palo Duro was an ideal site for a ranch. There was plenty of water and wood, shelter from the cold northers, and good grass. Goodnight drove the buffalo out of the canyon and stationed guards to prevent their return. With the backing of John Adair, a Scotsman, the JA Ranch, under the management of Goodnight, became one of the greatest in the Panhandle. Other ranches soon sprang up, among them Tom Bugbee's Quarter Circle T (1876), Hank Cresswell's Bar CC (1877) and Bates and Beals's LX.[4]

III   *The LX Ranch*

In July 1877 Charlie Siringo rode into the Panhandle with a herd owned by D. T. Beals and W. H. ("Deacon") Bates. The herd, about 2,500 longhorn steers, was purchased at Dodge City, where Siringo "hired out" to Beals. The crew consisted of Deacon Bates, who was to choose the ranch site; the foreman, Bill Allen; and eight other men, besides the cook, O. M. Johnson. Each man had six horses in his string. Siringo's horses were colorfully named: Comanche, Allison, Last Chance, Creeping Moses, Damfido, and Beat-and-be-Damned.[5]

The location of the LX Ranch differed little from that of other Panhandle ranches; the entire process seems very casual. When the herd reached a stream called Blue Creek, a temporary camp was located. Bates and Siringo rode ahead to locate a permanent range, one large enough for at least 50,000 cattle. The first town they reached was Tascosa, a small settlement on the Canadian River, later to become a riproaring cow town. When Siringo first saw Tascosa it consisted of only a half-dozen Mexican families and a store owned by Howard and Rinehart. The stock of goods in the store consisted of three barrels of whiskey and a half-dozen boxes of soda crackers.

From Tascosa, Bates and Siringo rode down the Canadian River twenty-five miles to the mouth of Pitcher Creek, where a man named Pitcher ran a store, selling only whiskey and tobacco, and traded for furs and buffalo hides. About a mile east of Pitcher Creek Bates chose a site for the ranch later known as the LX. In 1883 Siringo stated that the Wheeler post office stood where the LX headquarters had been. Not longer after Siringo wrote, however, the Wheeler post office was done away with. Present-day Wheeler is not in the same location.

The range itself was to extend twenty miles up the river, twenty miles down the river, twenty miles south to the foot of the Staked Plains, and twenty miles north to the foot of what was called the North Staked Plains. Thus the ranch covered an area about forty miles square—about 1,600 square miles, more than a million acres.

The herd was moved to this area and turned loose to fatten on the

buffalo grass. Bates then traveled to Granada, Colorado, the site of
the original Bates and Beals ranch, to supervise the moving of their
thousands of fine shorthorn cattle to the Panhandle. Beals and
Erskine Clement, another partner, remained in Dodge City, Kansas,
buying longhorns for the ranch.[6]

IV   The Buffalo

In 1877, although the slaughter of the buffalo had been going on
for several years, there were still buffalo on the plains. The first
herd that the Bates and Beals crew sighted was near the Cimarron
River, in "No Man's Land," now a part of Oklahoma. Siringo and
Bates rode ahead to kill a buffalo for fresh meat. When they were
within a mile of the herd, they tied their ponies in a gulch and
walked out on the open prairie straight toward the herd. At about a
hundred yards both men fired their Sharps rifles, killing two buffalo. The herd began bawling and milling around the fallen
animals. Siringo states that he was scared and wanted to run back to
his horse, but Bates walked into the milling herd, shooing them out
of the way with his hat. It was a trait of the buffalo, according to
Siringo, to run from a horseman but to pay no attention to a man on
foot.[7]

A universal cowboy sport, if one can believe reminiscences of old-
time cowboys, was the roping of buffalo—usually a sport to the buffalo and a disaster to the cowboy, because the mature buffalo was
about twice as large as a longhorn steer. Siringo records such an experience, giving the story a different twist. One evening when he
was in camp he made up his mind to go buffalo hunting with others
of the crew. But, seeing some steers leaving the herd, he first rode
out to turn them back. On his way back to camp he saw a small herd
of buffalo, running because of the shooting of the other cowboys.

Siringo, forgetting that he had left his rifle and pistol in camp,
took off after the herd. By the time he caught up, he missed his
guns; so he decided to rope a buffalo. He chose a heifer calf, which
immediately began to bellow. Its mother broke out of the herd and
took after Siringo, who could not get away because his rope was tied
fast to the saddle horn. Finally the cow rejoined the herd, leaving
Siringo with the calf. He tried several times to kill it by throwing it
hard and breaking its neck, but without success. Finally he dismounted, threw the calf, and tied it with the silk sash which he used
for a belt, and cut its throat with a dull pocket knife.[8]

Charles Goodnight was able to keep the buffalo out of his cattle herds by placing guards at strategic points in the Palo Duro Canyon. Other Panhandle ranches were not so fortunate. During the first winter LX herds were in the Panhandle, some of the steers followed the buffalo herds. Siringo, then on "sign" camp duty, saw the great herd of buffalo migrating south. He states that there was a solid band of buffalo, from one to three miles wide, which spent three days and nights crossing the Canadian River. During the daytime he could look to the north, across the Canadian breaks, a distance of thirty miles, and see "a black streak of living flesh" coming down off the North Plains. Trailing a bunch of steers which had followed the herd, Siringo found them with the buffalo at Amarillo Lake, where Siringo estimated there were at least a million buffalo. The herds were being exterminated rapidly, however, and the winter of 1877 - 1878 was probably the last ꞏwinter that such a large herd migrated across the Canadian to the south.[9]

V *Cowboys and Outlaws*

In the 1870s, a period of rapid expansion of the Range Cattle Industry, employers could not be as careful in the hiring of cowboys as they were during the next decade. Because of the need for men, they asked few questions about a man's past, especially if he had drifted in from somewhere else. Consequently, they sometimes hired cowboys who were "on the dodge," men who were on the wanted posters.

One of the legendary characters of the Panhandle, one who greatly impressed Siringo, was William C. ("Outlaw Bill") Moore, one of the LX managers. There has been considerable difference of opinion as to the worth of Moore to the LX. Siringo believed him to be a crook, but at the same time he admitted that the owners of the LX were careful in their hiring of general managers. After Moore left the LX Siringo himself was recommended for the position by Beals, but the other members of the firm thought him too wild and reckless for such a responsible position.[10]

Moore rode into the LX headquarters one day on a broken-down cow pony and was hired as a cowboy. When a vacancy occurred, he was made general manager. Siringo considered Moore a natural-born leader of men, one of the best cowmen in the West. He could get more work out of a gang of cowboys than anyone else Siringo had ever seen. But his history is one of almost continual outlawry.

He had been the manager of the Swan Cattle Company of Cheyenne, Wyoming, before coming to the LX. There he shot and killed his Negro coachman, made his getaway from the pursuing officers, and finally stopped at the LX.

The general managers of large ranches with absentee owners sometimes were, like Moore, unscrupulous. Siringo says that Moore, as soon as he became general manager, began "feathering his own nest" by putting his own brand on LX cattle, after having established a ranch at Coldwater Spring, in No Man's Land. Two LX cowboys were in with Moore on the cattle thefts. Siringo says he was asked to join the elite group, but he refused. After about three years Moore sold his ranch and cattle for $70,000, quit the LX, and established a ranch in the American Valley in New Mexico. His stay there, however, was short. He killed two men there and again became a fugitive. Many years later, Siringo, on a Pinkerton investigation in Alaska, met Moore, who was living there under an assumed name.

Moore, himself, was none too particular about the men he hired. In 1878, E. W. Parker and his large, well-armed crew of Star Route mail surveyors came to the ranch headquarters. The secret mission of this crew was to survey the first mail route in the Panhandle, from Ft. Elliot, in Wheeler County, which was at that time being organized, to Las Vegas, New Mexico, a distance of about three hundred miles. The LX Ranch headquarters at that time became Wheeler post office. But when the mail route crew, its mission not publicized, rode into ranch headquarters, about half of Moore's men, thinking the strangers were Texas Rangers in disguise, "hit the trail for tall timber," many of them on stolen ponies.

Moore influenced somewhat the equipment of the cowboy of the High Plains. He had learned the cattle trade in California, where the "center fire," or single-girth, saddle was used. The California cowboy used a seventy-five-foot rawhide lariat (also called a riata, both terms coming from the Spanish *la reata*), which he "dallied" or "dally-weltered" around the saddle horn when he roped. In other words, he merely wrapped the rope once or twice around the saddle horn, so that if he caught something he could not handle, he could turn it loose. The term "dally-welter" is a Texan corruption, one of many, of the Spanish phrase *dar la vuelta*, which means, roughly, "to give a turn." Also, Texas cowboys, being used to brush-country riding, used two cinches (girths) on their saddles (called "rim-fire" saddles) and roped with a short rope tied fast to the saddle horn. Siringo says he never saw Moore lose his saddle, because Moore was used to the single girth, but many of the Texas cowboys, using center-fire saddles for the first time, had their saddles jerked over sideways.[11]

VI *Ranching Methods*

Methods of ranching underwent a great change in the transition from the brush country to the plains. Especially important was the control of large areas of land, either by ownership or lease. The LX, as were other Panhandle ranches, was involved in this process for many years. Siringo, being merely a cowboy, does not write of the problem. He does, however, describe some of the operational changes which had to be made in order to effect the transition from the brush country to the plains. Herding cattle in the thick brush was impossible; the cattle could not be seen, much less herded. On the plains, however, it was possible to keep the cattle together, to some extent. In the fall of 1877, after herds had been brought in from Colorado and Dodge City, all the LX cattle were thrown into one large herd. "Sign" camps were established around the entire ranch, along the boarders, about twenty-five or thirty miles apart.

Each camp housed two men; their duty was to see that no cattle drifted outside of the line of their "ride," which was halfway to the next camp on each side. If any cattle had crossed over the line during the night, the cowboys would trail them and bring them back. "Reading sign" thus was a necessary skill. The first winter Siringo and a cowboy named John Robinson were assigned to a sign camp south of the ranch headquarters, at the foot of the Staked Plains. Since cattle tend to drift south during a cold spell, the Texas norther, this assignment was the worst of the lot. Siringo and Robinson, however, had a "hogkilling time," hunting and chasing cows. They always had four or five different kinds of meat in camp.

VII *The Cow Hunt and the Roundup*

Because the range covered such a large area, over a million acres, it was possible for many cattle to stray, despite line riders. As a consequence, the large-scale roundup became the custom. But Moore was not content to depend only on roundups. In the spring of 1878 he put a crew in the field looking for strays. Siringo was a member of the outfit, which consisted of three cowboys and a cook, with a

well-filled chuck wagon. Each cowboy had two good horses; Siringo
also took his own horse, Whiskey Pete. The crew was to go wherever
they thought cattle had strayed. After an absence of seven weeks
they returned to ranch headquarters with eighteen stray steers.

Although Siringo's dates are vague, the two later books agree that
a general roundup was held in the Panhandle in March or April of
1878. Other sources agree.[12] All the ranches in the area banded
together and systematically rounded up all the cattle, distributing
them to their proper owners. This phase of the cowboy's work has
caught the imagination of pulp Western writers, as well as of
Western historians with imaginary saddle burns. Siringo's description is matter-of-fact; he seemed to consider the roundup a part of
the routine.

The LX crew consisted of about twenty-five cowboys; two well-
supplied chuck wagons provided their food. The central meeting
place was the little town of Tascosa, which was unable to cope with
its population explosion. Howard and Rinehart's store soon sold out
of liquor and sardines and crackers, and the town soon saw the need
for saloons and dance halls to relieve the wild and woolly cowboy of
his loose change. Outfits came from as far as the Arkansas River in
Southeastern Colorado and Southwestern Kansas.

The roundup started near Bascom, New Mexico, and continued
down the Canadian River to the Indian Territory Line. Many cattle
which had drifted during the winter were returned to their ranges.[13]

VIII   *Grass Fire!*

Siringo describes a prairie fire which he helped to put out in the
spring of 1878. One evening before bedtime the sky in the southeast
became red. A prairie grass fire, one of the greatest catastrophes of
the High Plains, was being driven by a strong southeast wind directly toward the LX ranch headquarters. Moore roused the cowboys
and led them in a swift gallop toward the big fire, in pitch darkness,
over all kinds of rough terrain. After a ride of about fifteen miles
they came to the fire, before which large herds of cattle were running.

Some of the larger animals were killed, the carcasses split open,
and ropes tied to the hind legs. If the fire was down in an arroyo,
where the tall blue-stem grass grew, it was allowed to burn its way
to a level place covered with short buffalo grass. There two cowboys
would drag a carcass along the line of the blaze, the one on the

burnt side with his rope short and the other, on the hot side, with his rope long. The wet carcass was dragged slowly along the blaze, putting out most of the fire. The remaining small, isolated blazes were beaten out by other cowboys with wet saddle blankets or green cowhides. After a carcass was worn out, another steer was killed and the process continued. The cowboys fought the fire until three o'clock the following afternoon, when it was brought under control and the ranch headquarters saved.[14]

IX *Straw Boss*

During the summer of 1878 Siringo was given his first responsibility as a straw boss, although by his own admission his responsibilities never rested very heavily on his shoulders. Steers had to be marketed, and, obviously, tame, fat steers were more marketable. After the long winter the steers were both wild and thin. Moore decided to close-herd the cattle during the summer, putting crews in the field, each with 2,500 to 3,000 cattle to herd together so that they would become tame and would be in better shape at the end of the summer. The main object of the close-herding was to keep the cattle from "chousing around," or running too much.

About the first of June, Moore gave Siringo the responsibility for a herd of 2,500 steers. His outfit consisted of a wagon and cook and four riders, each with five horses in his string. He was instructed to drift over the plains, going anywhere he wished, but the cattle were to be brought back fat before winter. The summer of 1878 was unusually wet, and scores of surface basins, or dry lakes, typical of the plains, were filled with water. The buffalo grass was exceptionally lush. Siringo says that if he ever really enjoyed life, it was that summer. There were no flies or mosquitoes, game was plentiful, and the atmosphere of the High Plains was balmy.

Near the last of July about 10,000 through cattle—cattle that had not been wintered on the plains—arrived from South Texas. To keep the wintered cattle from catching Texas fever, to which South Texas cattle were immune, Moore moved them all south of the Canadian, leaving the new arrivals, with the fever-carrying ticks, on the north side. The cause of Texas fever had not yet been determined, but quarantine until the cattle had wintered in colder climates had been proved effective. First frost usually killed the ticks on the bedding grounds.

Siringo was put in charge of all four herds of wintered cattle. His

job until late in the fall was to supervise all four herds, counting
each herd once a week to make sure none had strayed and keeping
the crews supplied with food. Siringo felt "somewhat important."[15]

The drive from the Panhandle to Dodge City was a relatively
short one, so that LX cattle could be marketed in the fall. In October 1878 Moore picked about 800 fat steers out of the wintered
herd and started them trailing for Dodge City. The rest of the herd
was turned loose on the winter range. Siringo wanted to go with the
herd and see the big city. So, after the hardest work was over,
Moore allowed Siringo to overtake the herd, which had been on the
trail for about fifteen days, and to help ship it to Chicago.

With another cowboy, John Ferris, Siringo, mounted on his
favorite horse, Whiskey Pete, struck out after the herd. There had
been an Indian uprising in the Indian Territory, and the cowboys
found Mead City and the store on Crooked Creek ransacked, the inhabitants driven away. Later they found out that three men had
been killed in the uprising. When they arrived in Dodge City they
found that the herd had not arrived. Siringo and Erskine Clement,
who was waiting in Dodge City, backtracked, finding the herd,
which had left the main trail in order to find water. The steers, in
two shipments, were loaded on a train for Chicago, Siringo being in
charge of the first shipment.

X   Cow Puncher

For the first time, Siringo says, he became a cow puncher, carrying a long pole with a spike on the end, a cow prod, to keep the
steers on their feet in the crowded cars. Later, he says, the term
"cow puncher" was applied to all cowboys.

The herd was unloaded at Burlington, Iowa, to be fed and
watered, and the cowboys had a two-day layover. They made
several trips to Burlington—a "swift city"—on the ferry.
Tradesmen, seeing their cowboy garb, including pistols, would not
take their money. Transportation, liquor, cigars, meals, and candy
were all free. Siringo felt somehow—a faint suspicion—that the
people of Burlington were trying to promote the shipment of cattle
by way of their city.

Just out of Burlington Siringo "came within an ace" of being
killed under the wheels of the train. A sleet storm was raging, and,
when the train stopped to take on coal, the three cow punchers left
the caboose and worked their way toward the engine, peering

through the cracks of the cattle cars to locate any steers which were down and get them on their feet again. About the time they reached the engine, the train started. The men started back to the caboose, on the run, on the walkway on top of the cattle cars, with Siringo bringing up the rear. As he jumped from one car to the next, Siringo, in high-heeled boots, slipped on the ice, falling flat on his back with his head and shoulders over the two-foot space between the cars. He grabbed the edge of the catwalk with his right hand, saving himself from falling between the cars.

XI   *The Big City*

Siringo's main reason for wanting to help with the cattle shipments was probably the good times to be had in the large city. Beals met the train at Chicago. After eating supper with Beals at the Palmer House, Siringo decided that the Palmer was "too rich for his blood" (his supper cost a dollar), and he rented a room at another hotel, the Irvine House, where the cost was $2 a night. Then, like a country boy come to town, Siringo, in Chicago for the first time, turned himself loose in the toughest part of the city.

In his cowboy garb, he was an easy mark. During the night he spent about $200. He estimated that at least $15 of that amount was spent on bootblacks, who seemed to know at a glance, from the "cut of his jib," that they had struck a bonanza.

The next morning, walking down the street, Siringo saw a dentist's sign, went in, and had $45 worth of dental work done. After the work was completed, he reached in his pocket and found that he was broke. The dentist, evidently impressed by Siringo's pistol and bowie knife, did not argue when Siringo promised to pay the bill the next day. Siringo borrowed another $100 from Beals, and, after putting the dentist's money aside, went out to see the sights again. The next morning the dentist was agreeably surprised at being paid—so surprised, in fact, that he invited Siringo to have lunch with him. After a few more days in the city, Siringo headed back to Dodge City and to the LX, about $100 in debt to Beals.[16]

During the next two years Siringo's work for the LX varied little from the routine of the first year. In the fall of 1879 he made the 1,100-mile trip to South Texas to see his mother, working his way south (even picking cotton for a while). The next spring he took a herd which the LX had bought from Charlie Word of Beeville to the Panhandle.[17]

The following fall (1880) Siringo became involved in the Billy the Kid controversy and the Lincoln County War. This range war was typical of the violence that accompanied the development of the Range Cattle Industry, and Siringo's experience with Billy the Kid, though not extensive, influenced him profoundly.

CHAPTER 5

An Era of Conflict

A S the Range Cattle Industry developed rapidly, cattle rustling, an extension of early-day mavericking, became an in-
creasingly important problem. Although it is difficult to determine
which faction was on the side of right in such diverse conflicts as the
Lincoln County, New Mexico, War and the Johnson County,
Wyoming, War, it is obvious that an important element in both
struggles was the ever-present cattle rustling which occurred
throughout the West. Siringo, while not deeply involved in the Lincoln County War, was a more than interested observer. And cattle
rustling, real or alleged, took him to Lincoln County.

In Outlaw Bill Moore Siringo had seen the thieving ranch
manager who put his own brand on his employers' cattle. In Henry
McCarty, or Henry Antrim, alias William H. Bonney, alias Billy the
Kid, he saw the outlaw killer who made raids on Panhandle ranches,
driving cattle out of the state to be sold. The folk hero - outlaw—
and Billy the Kid was a folk hero—has always been viewed by his
admirers as one who robs the unworthy rich for the benefit of the
worthy poor. And the cattle rustler was often excused by the belief
that the "cattle baron" obtained his large herds by unscrupulous
practices. So wrong—rustling—is added to other wrongs, so that
right might prevail! Such is the conclusion of the romanticists who
made a hero out of Henry McCarty.

If cattle raising was to be profitable, the control of rustling was
imperative. The Lincoln County War and the career of Billy the
Kid were not isolated incidents; they were symptoms, part of a
struggle taking place through a changing West. The end of the
open range was imminent. Cowmen, in order to control the land
they used, much of it public land, needed to get a legal title to it.
The Lincoln County War, the subject of many books, was essentially a power struggle, a war of economics. It marked a transition

from extralegal control to a society emphasizing law and order.
Early settlers, especially cattlemen on a rapidly expanding frontier,
often took the law into their own hands. As the country developed,
however, legal governments were established and politically powerful men such as Charles Goodnight worked toward the suppression
of crime, including cattle rustling. An important result of the breaking up of Billy the Kid's gang in Lincoln County, even though rustling was not a primary issue, was the discouraging of rustling.

I   Siringo to Lincoln County

And it was Billy the Kid's theft of Panhandle cattle that took
Charlie Siringo into Lincoln County, an interested observer but one
unwilling to take sides in the struggle. The reason for Siringo's
reluctance is an enigma. Jim East, later a Potter County sheriff,
doubted his bravery. Others have thought he was involved with
Billy the Kid. Possibly he felt bound by the reason he was sent to
New Mexico—to recover stolen cattle. Also, he may have felt a close
affinity for the Kid; their backgrounds were similar, and they
looked alike.

Siringo, like every other old-timer who was within a hundred
miles of Lincoln County during the trouble, wrote much about Billy
the Kid. Like the works of all of the old-timers, his account of the
Kid's early days was based largely on Pat Garrett's *Authentic Life of
Billy the Kid*, ghost written by a newspaperman named Ash Upson.

It is ironic that the account of the Kid's life that was standard for
seventy years was by the Kid's killer. Manuel Otero, ex-governor of
New Mexico, reproached Siringo for copying from Garrett. Yet entire paragraphs from Otero's book, *The Real Billy the Kid*, were
copied almost verbatim from Garrett.[1]

One can discount the value of Siringo's *History of "Billy the
Kid"*, especially the information about the Kid's early life, but the
same thing can be said about virtually all of the early books about
the Kid. Ramon Adams has spent many years in pursuit of the
legend of Billy the Kid and has succeeded in stripping away much
of the myth.[2] The value of Siringo's "history," in his Billy the Kid
book and in his three autobiographical books, lies in his accounts of
his personal slight involvement and his observation of some of the
peripheral events of the struggle. And Siringo's part in the struggle
was merely an extension of his responsibility to the LX. His observa-
tions add to a great mass of material descriptive of a way of life that

was passing away. The open range as a way of economic life was doomed; the development of ranches, fenced and watered by inventions promoted by American ingenuity, was eventually to dominate cattle raising. However much one might like or dislike the change, the change did come about. Romantics writing about the modern cowboy cannot alter the facts.

II   Siringo and the "Cowboy Bad Man"

Siringo's actions in Lincoln County must have been colored by his attitude toward the "cowboy bad man." In an interview just before his death Siringo expressed the belief that few bad men were really as bad as they were painted. Their deeds were exaggerated by rumor. (Today he probably would say the exaggeration was done by the makers of myth and folklore.) Most of the outlaws, he said, were good fellows at heart, men who simply had not learned to control their impulses, although this really was no excuse for their outlawry. Usually they were victims of their environment, but, nevertheless, Siringo did not approve of their becoming heroes. They were men who, after getting into one desperate scrape, went from bad to worse on false trails, hoping to "save their skins." He did not judge them; he merely tried to understand them.[3] And he spent many years as a Pinkerton detective pursuing and apprehending them.

I believe that Siringo felt that his and Billy the Kid's lives were similar. Both were orphaned early, both had stepfathers, both had Irish mothers, and both were "on their own" early in life. In his early—and even his later—years Siringo was as hotheaded as the Kid and as free with his knife. In his years as a detective Siringo many times used as an alias the name "Lee Roy," which appeared in an early dime novel as the Kid's name. Later Siringo named his son Lee Roy. Even stranger is the fact that the two men looked alike. Several times Siringo was mistaken for the Kid.[4] A comparison of a picture of Siringo made in 1891 with a purported picture of Billy the Kid made in 1876 shows a marked resemblance between the two men. In fact, I believe that the pictures are of the same person—Siringo—although I cannot explain James S. Guyer's believing his picture was that of Billy the Kid.[5]

At least, it seems evident that Siringo was sympathetic toward Billy the Kid. He wanted no part in the Kid's capture. And he himself often lived very close to that borderline which he described, that is, the point where a man commits that one rash act which puts him outside the law. It is not known whether Siringo ever killed a man, but his own accounts reveal occasions when he came very near to killing, in circumstances which would have made him an outlaw.

Siringo was associated with Billy the Kid only once, during the fall of 1878, just after the bloodiest part of the Lincoln County War, when the Kid and his gang were camped near the LX ranch head-quarters. They had stolen a herd of horses in New Mexico and had brought them to the Panhandle to be sold. The tradition is that the ranchers around Tascosa agreed to leave the gang alone if the gang would leave their cattle alone. The outlaws were around the LX and Tascosa for several weeks, until the horses were sold.

Siringo, having just made his first trip to Chicago, arrived at the ranch headquarters and found the Kid there. When the cook rang the supper bell, the strangers were the first ones at the long supper table. Siringo was seated beside the "good-natured" Billy the Kid. When supper was over, Siringo passed around a box of fine Havana cigars which he had bought in Chicago. He stuck his own cigar into a fine meerschaum cigar holder, which struck the fancy of the Kid. When the Kid asked permission to try the holder out, Siringo gave it to him. In return the Kid presented Siringo with an autographed copy of a "finely-bound" novel which he had just finished reading.[6] During the next few weeks the two became "quite chummy," according to Siringo.[7]

In Siringo's introduction to his *History of "Billy the Kid"*, 1920, he declared that he was capable of writing a "true and unvar-nished" history of Billy the Kid, since he was personally acquainted with him and "assisted" in his capture by furnishing sheriff Pat Garrett with three of his fighting cowboys. The last statement was probably made with tongue in cheek, because Siringo obviously was not eager to see the Kid captured. Siringo lists as sources men who were active for or against the Kid, men whom he had interviewed. He seems, however, to have relied mainly upon Pat Garrett and his ghost writer, Ash Upson.[8] Although Siringo refused personally to help in the hunt, he did eventually contribute very much to the legend of the Kid. Ramon Adams gives Siringo credit for the legend's being widely distributed and publicized because Siringo's books were popular and frequently printed (he accepts Siringo's es-timate that "nearly a million copies" of *A Texas Cow Boy* were sold, leaving out the "nearly").[9] Certainly Siringo's books were widely read.

Cattle rustling involved Siringo in the final events of Billy the

Kid's life, although his involvement was peripheral. Late in the fall of 1880 Siringo was called in to ranch headquarters by Moore to head a crew of men who were to go to New Mexico and recover cattle the Kid's gang had stolen from Panhandle herds.

III   *The Search for Rustlers*

The cattlemen along the Canadian River had hired Frank Stewart to scout for the cattle in New Mexico. He had returned during the summer and had reported that Billy the Kid was making a regular business of selling Panhandle cattle to an old Irishman named Pat Coghlin, who ran a slaughterhouse on his ranch near Fort Stanton. So the Panhandle cattlemen made up a "crowd" between them and sent Stewart with the men, giving him orders to go to Coghlin's ranch and recover all the cattle wearing Panhandle brands. According to Siringo, instead of going to the ranch, Stewart turned back, never getting within forty miles of the ranch. Stewart claimed that Coghlin had sent him word that if the cattle were recovered Stewart would have to take some hot lead with them. Stewart turned back because he thought he did not have enough men.[10]

Moore, disgusted with the Stewart fiasco, decided to "rig up" an outfit of his own to recover the cattle. He chose Siringo to head the crew, which consisted of a cook driving a chuck wagon pulled by four good mules, Siringo, and his "fighting crew": James East, Lee Hall, Lon Chambers, Cal Polk, and Frank Clifford, alias Big Foot Wallace. Each man had an extra horse except Siringo, who had two. Moore, hoping to save feed, felt that it would be cheaper for Siringo to buy more horses in New Mexico.

It should be noted that Moore gave Siringo very specific orders. He was to stay in New Mexico until he either recovered the cattle or broke the LX Company. Moore would keep them supplied with money as long as the company had a nickel left. Siringo was to recover the cattle first. Then if he thought he could capture Billy the Kid he was to do so. He could hire all the men he needed, but the main goal was to recover the cattle.

At Tascosa Siringo's crew met Stewart, who had succeeded in raising a crew from Littlefield's LIT Ranch and two smaller ranches. In his earliest account Siriingo states that Stewart was in charge of all the men except Siringo's crew. Later, he says that Bob Roberson was in charge of the Littlefield crew and that Stewart was working by himself. Which account is accurate cannot be determined. It is possible that the early book, in which Siringo was most unkind to Stewart, is more accurate. He became more tactful (or cautious) in his criticism of other men in his later books. On the other hand, it is possible that in the later books he corrected some "windies" told in A *Texas Cow Boy*. At any rate, Siringo says that after the crew got "strung out" Stewart took the mail line buckboard and went ahead to Las Vegas, New Mexico, to spend a week or so with his "solid girl."

IV *Siringo the "Leader"*

The next incident in Siringo's account gives a strange picture of employer-employee relationships. It is not known where early LX records are, if indeed they exist, and Siringo's story cannot be checked for accuracy. The story would be even stranger were it not for the fact that Moore, the general manager, was not especially interested in saving the LX's money.

When the gang arrived at San Lorenzo, New Mexico, Siringo "mounted a buckboard" and headed for Las Vegas to buy supplies, which were to be delivered at Anton Chico, twenty-five miles south of Las Vegas; the crew was to wait for him there. Siringo was supposed to buy supplies for Bob Roberson's men also.

When he arrived at Las Vegas, however, Siringo found that there was no corn to be bought; a snowstorm had delayed the freight trains. Because one merchant was expecting several carloads of corn at any time, Siringo decided to help Stewart hold the town down. He wrote a letter to the men at Anton Chico, telling them he might be delayed several days, and then settled in to play his favorite card game, monte, losing the $300 Moore had given him, as well as about $100 of Roberson's money. When the corn arrived, he found a merchant who would take an order on the LX and bought the supplies. Siringo admits that he hated to use the company's credit so soon after leaving the ranch, but he felt that was the best he could do under the circumstances. And one can understand why Siringo was not made general manager when Moore left. Siringo and Stewart rode to the camp at Anton Chico, where the men, thinking Siringo had plenty of money, had run up a considerable debt at local stores. Siringo again "gave more orders" on the LX company.[11]

V *What Happened?*

There is some confusion as to what happened next, even in Siringo's books. In the later accounts he states that the crew left for White Oaks because the Kid's gang had stolen some horses at Anton Chico and had headed in that direction. Pat Garrett rode into their camp the next morning, asked for men for a posse, and received three men from Siringo and two men from Roberson, Stewart going along of his own accord.

But the original account in *A Texas Cow Boy* seems more likely. It states that when Siringo and Stewart reached Anton Chico, Barney Mason, one of Garrett's deputies, was waiting there with a note for Stewart, telling him that Garrett wished to see him in Las Vegas on important business. Stewart immediately started back for Las Vegas. Siringo and crew started for White Oaks a few days later. At Llewellyn Wells they were overtaken by Stewart, Garrett, and Barney Mason.

They came, says Siringo, with a cut-and-dried scheme to get the big reward offered for the Kid. Garrett knew that the Kid and his gang had been at Anton Chico and had left for Fort Sumner a few days before, worn out from being chased all over the country. Siringo believed that Garrett had promised Stewart half the reward to go "in cahoots" with him.

Siringo writes that after breakfast Stewart "broke the ice" by telling a lie. He stated that the Kid was on the way to Mexico with a bunch of Panhandle cattle and that every man in the outfit except just enough to take the wagons to White Oaks should go with Garrett to overtake the outlaws. Stewart lied, Siringo thought, because he knew what Siringo's orders were. Siringo and the other men, knowing Stewart, doubted his word, thinking that the whole thing was a "put up job" to gain the reward.

Roberson and Siringo talked the matter over alone and decided, just in case Stewart's tale were true, to lend Garrett and Stewart a few men, but not enough to cripple the original crew if they found a lead on lost cattle. Consequently, Siringo lent Garrett three men—Jim East, Lon Chambers, and Lee Hall—while Roberson supplied him with Bob Williams, Louis Bausman, and Tom Emory. Siringo, Roberson, and the rest of the crew continued in a snow-storm to White Oaks.[12]

Jim East, one of Siringo's cowboys, gave an entirely different version of the story. In interviews with J. Evetts Haley in 1927 and
1928 he stated that Siringo arrived at Anton Chico broke and
without food. According to East, Stewart had no authority in the
crew, but Garrett and Mason rode into camp and asked for help in
catching the Kid and his gang, who were driving a herd of cattle.
According to East, Roberson turned tail and declined to go, as did
Siringo, and the two took the wagons down to White Oaks and
holed up for the winter. He said that Siringo gave no explanation
for his action, nor did he give Garrett any men. Those who went
with Garrett went of their own accord.[13]

I doubt the trustworthiness of East's information. Garrett and
Siringo agree as to the men who went along, and they do not agree
with East. Moreover, in a letter to Siringo, written in 1920, East said
that "after a lapse of forty years, one's memory may slip a cog."[14]
Perhaps by 1927 or 1928, two or three cogs had slipped.

Pat Garrett in his account states that he sent Mason to Stewart's
"posse," asking Stewart to meet him in Las Vegas. Stewart went,
and the two men agreed to work together. Garrett, Mason, and
Stewart rode after the "posse" and overtook them at Llewellyn
Wells, where Stewart called for volunteers. The account is very
much in agreement with Siringo's, except that Garrett was under
the impression that Stewart was in charge of the entire crew, which
was not really a "posse."[15] I believe Siringo's first account is essentially accurate.

Siringo's reason for not going with the posse seems valid. Capture
of Billy the Kid's gang was secondary; it is amusing that Siringo's
men were in Anton Chico (Siringo was in Las Vegas) when the Kid
and his gang walked into the town and left on horseback. The men
in the crew made no attempt to capture anyone. The Kid's escape,
even an escape afoot, made a good story for them to tell Siringo and
Stewart when they arrived. Siringo and the crew knew that the
Kid's gang had no cattle; they were lucky to be mounted.

VI   *The Kid's Capture*

As Roberson, Siringo, and the rest of the men drove through
the snowstorm toward White Oaks, they passed the still smoking
ruins of the Jim Greathouse road ranch, fired by the posse which
had failed to capture the Kid there. This posse, led by Deputy
Sheriff Jim Carlyle, had surrounded the ranch. Carlyle had gone

into the ranch house to talk to the Kid and had been killed by the Kid while trying to escape through the window. Greathouse was held as a hostage by the posse, and when someone in the posse accidentally fired a shot, Carlyle, thinking Greathouse had been killed, jumped through a window. The Kid, agreeing with Carlyle about Greathouse, shot and killed Carlyle. Greathouse survived, and the Kid and his gang escaped that night.

Siringo and his crew did winter in and near White Oaks, as Jim East told J. Evetts Haley. First they camped near the edge of town, then rented a building in the town itself. Two White Oaks merchants gave them unlimited credit for "grub" and horse feed. In order to have fresh meat they followed the "old Texas custom" of butchering another man's beef. Some of their neighbors thought this custom immoral, but they never failed to help eat up the beef. Siringo says that the only brand they looked at was "fat."

The first word Siringo had of the posse's activities was brought in by three Panhandle cowboys, Lee Hall, Lon Chambers, and Louis Bausman. The Kid had been captured and two of his gang killed. The rest of the posse had gone with Garrett to take the Kid to the penitentiary at Santa Fe, via Las Vegas, for safekeeping. Finally all the men except Stewart rejoined the crew. During the next few days there was much speculation about what each man would do with his share of the reward which Stewart was supposedly going to bring back to White Oaks. However, when Stewart finally arrived at the camp, he told them that the reward money was already spent. Siringo says Stewart ordered Roberson's crew back to the Panhandl and took off for Las Vegas just in time to save his own hide. Bob Roberson, either on his own or because of Stewart's orders—accounts differ—decided to go home. With him went Jim East, Lee Hall, and Cal Polk. East, says Siringo, wanted to go back and run for sheriff of Oldham County. Siringo decided to wait until spring and look for strayed LX cattle.[16]

VII *Rustlers*

About the first of February Siringo set out to do what he was sent to New Mexico to do. He had received word in the meantime from Moore to continue looking for LX cattle and to bring them back if it took him two years. He and Tom Emory rode out to Fort Stanton to examine the hides in Pat Coghlin's slaughterhouse, taking witnesses along. They found several hides from freshly killed LX cattle. Storing them for future use as evidence, Siringo rode to Las Cruces and interviewed Coghlin, the "King of Tularosa." Coghlin, after he was told of Siringo's intention of searching the range for other LX cattle, asked him not to stir up his cattle until spring, promising not to butcher any more LX cattle. Siringo agreed. He rode back to Coghlin's ranch and spent the night.

The next morning he arose and started back to White Oaks. The Mexican foreman told Siringo of a shortcut over the mountains and consented to send one of the hands to start him on the trail. Siringo, who was riding a large work mule, decided the mountain route would be the best and thanked the foreman for his help.

About an hour after his guide left him, Siringo decided to take another shortcut. Just as he turned off the trail someone fired three shots at him in quick succession. The mule lunged forward, slipping on the ice-covered ground. She fell on her side, throwing Siringo over an eight-foot cliff. He grabbed his pistol, which was hanging in its holster over the saddle horn, as he left the saddle. With pistol cocked, he lay quiet for a few moments, waiting for the bushwhackers to show up. He then crawled up the cliff just in time to see two men running over a ridge a few hundred yards away.

He found the mule a little way up the trail, wounded in the breast. The other two bullets had passed through the cantle of his saddle and through his blanket. Since the mule was not badly wounded, Siringo rode her on to White Oaks. More than thirty years later Siringo's friend John F. Meadows of Tularosa told him that Coghlin had hired the Mexicans to kill him to prevent him from appearing as a witness at any future prosecution.

Siringo had made a bad error in judgment when he trusted Coghlin. After about a month he received a letter from George Nesbeth, a friend living on the Coghlin ranch, stating that Coghlin was butchering LX cattle as fast as he could, hoping to get them all butchered before spring. Siringo and "Big Foot Wallace" rode to Fort Stanton and searched the Coghlin slaughterhouse, finding five freshly butchered hides carrying the LX brand. Siringo wrote a letter to Moore, giving him all the details and advising him to prosecute Coghlin. Then he and Big Foot rode to the Coghlin ranch where, after an argument with Bill Gentry, the foreman, they cut eight LX steers out of the herd. Then they returned to White Oaks, taking the LX steers, as well as one wearing Coghlin's brand. The latter steer, with a fat hog which they had butchered before leaving the ranch, furnished them with meat for some time.

Siringo got his outfit together and started for the home ranch, rounding up Panhandle cattle as he went. They went through the Patos Mountains to Los Palos Springs and then to Roswell, on the Pecos River. There they laid over a week while John Chisum was preparing for the spring roundup on his Jinglebob range. They followed the Chisum roundup, taking charge of the two LX cattle found. While camped near the present site of Carlsbad, the men learned that Billy the Kid had killed his two guards, Bell and Olinger, at Lincoln, and had escaped. While the small herd was near Fort Sumner, Siringo rode to Sunnyside, six miles from Sumner, for supplies. It was there that he was mistaken for Billy the Kid. The crew lay over at Fort Sumner for two nights to take in the Mexican fandangoes.

At Fort Sumner Siringo almost met Billy the Kid again. The dances were held at the Maxwell home, where the Kid was later killed. The Kid was in the building while the dance was going on, unknown to most of the dancers. Siringo had danced several times with Mrs. Charlie Bowdre, the young Mexican widow of one of Billy's gang who had been killed by Garrett's posse. When the dance broke up, Siringo went with Mrs. Bowdre to her two-room adobe house, where he tried to persuade her to allow him to come in and talk awhile. Despite his insistence, she would not consent. A year later Mrs. Bowdre told Siringo that the Kid was inside the room, reading. Siringo noticed that she waited until he turned the corner before she entered.

Leaving Fort Sumner, Siringo and his crew went east toward Portales Lake on the west side of the Staked Plains. They camped one night at Stinking Springs, sleeping in the rock house where Billy the Kid and his gang were captured after holding out for a day and night without food or water. Chambers showed them the spot where Charlie Bowdre fell and where the battle took place. At Portales Lake they pitched camp at the cave where Billy the Kid had his headquarters while stealing LX cattle. The crew went east, through Yellow House Canyon, gathering strays as they went. After driving the cattle for two days and nights without water they came to Walter Dyer's house at the head of the Palo Duro Canyon, the first habitation they had seen since leaving Fort Sumner. They arrived at the LX Ranch with 2,500 head of cattle, after an absence of seven months.[17]

Siringo arrived at the LX on June 22, 1881; three weeks later, on July 14, 1881, Billy the Kid was killed by Pat Garrett at Pete Maxwell's house at Fort Sumner. In the meantime Moore had commissioned John Poe, the representative of the Canadian River Cattle Association, to prosecute Pat Coghlin for slaughtering LX cattle. Poe arrived in New Mexico in time to be a witness to the shooting of the Kid, as related in his small volume *The Death of Billy the Kid.* He spent his time recovering other cattle, as well as instituting, with the aid of Pat Garrett, prosecutions such as that of Coghlin.

VIII   *Aftermath*

About the middle of October 1881 Poe sent word for Siringo and Lon Chambers to come to Lincoln, New Mexico, to testify in the trial of Coghlin, set for November 7. Siringo was commissioned by the LX to spend the winter scouting along the Texas Pacific Railroad, at the foot of the South Staked Plains, for strayed LX cattle. By night the two men rode into the ranch headquarters of a man named Cline, near Lincoln, where they were to meet Poe. Coghlin, however, had "smelled a rat" and had applied for a change of venue to Dona Ana County; the change was granted. Poe instructed Siringo to appear at La Mesilla on the first Monday in April 1882 for the trial of Coghlin.

So Siringo, on the trail of information about Billy the Kid as well as on the trail of stray cattle, started back for Texas, mounted on a horse named Croppy and using a horse named Buckshot for a pack horse. He stopped at Roswell and rode out to Pat Garrett's ranch. Garrett was in Dallas, but Siringo found Ash Upson, who was living with Garrett, there. Upson had been instructed to meet Garrett at Pecos Station, on the Texas Pacific Railroad, on a certain day, and Siringo decided to make the trip with him. It was on this trip that Ash Upson, who had known Billy and his family since Billy was a small child, told Siringo the highly inaccurate "facts" of the life of the Kid.

The two men spent New Year's Day at Toyah, where Siringo won a "turkey shoot" for a pretty girl. Siringo then went on a scouting expedition along the Texas Pacific Railroad, starting at a proper time toward La Mesilla to appear in court. In Big Springs he lay in bed for two days with a high fever; he got out of bed, still ill, to continue the trip. At dark the first day a norther blew up, and he took refuge in a section house, where he found out that he was "broke out" with smallpox. He rode to the next section house, with his face covered, and continued riding from section house to section house until he reached Toyah. The doctor pronounced the danger of contagion past, and Siringo spent several days in the Alvarado Hotel at Toyah, where a pretty girl, "Miss Beulah," acted as his nurse. Finally he reached La Mesilla in time for the trial; Coghlin pleaded guilty and was fined two hundred and fifty dollars. Poe brought a $10,000 damage suit against Coghlin, but Siringo never found out the result of the suit.

On the trip back to Texas, Siringo, still interested in Billy the Kid, rode part of the way with cowboy Charlie Wall, who had witnessed the escape of Billy the Kid. From him Siringo found out, he thought, how the Kid killed his two guards and escaped. He "laid over" a few days at Lincoln, New Mexico, where he heard the "true account" of the death of Billy the Kid from the men involved: Pat Garrett, John W. Poe, and Kip McKinney. After staying in White Oaks a few days with friends, Siringo returned to the LX Ranch, having been gone for eight months and having ridden about three thousand miles.[18]

Siringo placed great importance upon his acquaintance with Billy the Kid and his part in the Kid's capture. He emphasized first the Kid's rustling as the reason he had a part in the chase. Siringo was in sympathy with the Kid's revolt against society, and he liked the Kid personally, but he also felt that it was his duty to recover the cattle which the Kid had stolen. Siringo did not join Garrett's posse because the Kid did not have any cattle with him; Siringo had been sent to New Mexico to recover cattle. And it seems obvious that Siringo had great sympathy for the Kid. It is very likely that the detective work which Siringo did on the New Mexico trip influenced him later to become a detective. He also saw the approaching end of the open range and the imminent changes of the cattle country from the "free open range system" to a fenced-in ranching system. The great change in an environment which he thought was almost perfect influenced his giving up cowboy life.

CHAPTER 6

End of the Open Range

INFLUENCES that were at work in Lincoln County, New Mexico, and in the Panhandle during the early 1880s were also at work all over the West. The first five years of the decade were filled with change. Law and order were gradually coming into the Great Plains area; rustling was more dangerous than it had ever been. The era of the open range was just about over; the Panhandle of Texas, at least, was becoming "crowded." During the first three years after the establishment of Fort Elliott there were eighteen big ranches set up in the Panhandle; in six years, there were twenty-four; in twelve years, there were thirty-three.[1] Besides being crowded with cowmen, the range was gradually being settled by "fool hoe-men," farmers who sought to farm on land much of which was suitable only for grazing.

There began a concentrated effort on the part of the big cattlemen of the Panhandle to acquire all the land possible and to fence it in. Since Texas owned her own lands, certificates had been granted to railroads as subsidy and to corporations and individuals for services, such as surveying, rendered to the state. The certificates could be located by the grantee on any of the unclaimed domain. The firm of Gunter, Munson, and Summerfield, surveyors and locators, of Sherman, Texas, did much of the surveying of the Panhandle, locating one certificate for another, taking their pay in kind. The firm practically cornered the land market. Charles Goodnight bought from them, locating his land in crazy-quilt fashion all over the Palo Duro Canyon.[2] Practically all Panhandle ranchers followed Goodnight's lead. Beals and Bates bought up all land on the LX range which bordered on streams or took in watering places such as lakes or springs, purchasing land from Gunter, Munson, and Summerfield and from the state. The Capitol Syndicate's XIT

Ranch also took up about three million acres of land in the Panhandle.[3]

If the rancher acquired title to land on the water and made sure that his land surrounded school land, he was able to graze the school land. It was this practice of Goodnight and other cattlemen of the Panhandle that led to the controversy over the Land Board Act of 1883, which provided for the competitive sale of as many as seven sections to an individual. It also provided that ranch lands be leased to cattlemen on a competitive basis for not less than four cents an acre. The result was that the cattlemen, who already recognized boundaries for their ranges, did not bid on each other's lands; each cattleman bid the minimum on the land which he was already grazing. The Land Board opposed this practice, without success.[4]

Barbed wire moved into the Panhandle in the early eighties, putting an end to free grazing. The first fences were drift fences, built to hold cattle out of (or in) a certain range. The most famous was one built by cooperating Panhandle ranchers north of the Canadian River in 1882. The first big enclosure was put up by the T Anchor Ranch in 1881 and 1882. By 1885 most of the Panhandle was fenced in.[5] The cattle industry saw the end of a great era; in order for ranching to survive, many adaptations had to be made. Many cattlemen and cowboys considered that when the land was fenced in the "glee and the glow" of a relatively free life were gone; Siringo was among them.

The LX Company had established a steer ranch in the Indian Territory just south of Caldwell, Kansas, which had become a shipping point. Later the company bought a small horse ranch near Caldwell. Soon after coming back from New Mexico Siringo began to make trail drives to Caldwell. He relates little of what happened during the years between 1881 and 1883; most of the work was merely routine. On the horse ranch near Caldwell, in 1883, Siringo conceived the idea of writing *A Texas Cow Boy*, a monument to the passing of the open range. Siringo liked Caldwell, "the Queen City of the Border," as well as a couple of young ladies there; he decided to locate in Caldwell.

He bought some lots and contracted for a house to be built for his mother. He arranged for a special job with Beals, feeding and taking care of about 200 ponies on the horse ranch. As there were plenty of fat ponies to ride, Siringo often rode to Caldwell to see the girls—and his mother.

About March 1, 1883, he met Mamie Lloyd, girl friend of May Beals, a niece of David T. Beals. Three days later they were engaged, three days after that they were married, and three days after the wedding Siringo was on his way to the LX in charge of a crew of men. He attended roundups on the Red and Pease Rivers, the crew arriving back at the LX about July 1 with 3,000 head of cattle. On September 1 Siringo was back in Caldwell with a herd of 800 fat steers.

Beals ordered him back to the LX for another herd; this order did not suit Siringo because he had been in Caldwell for only a few days. He started to go back, even going so far as to load the chuck wagon. Suddenly he turned the crew over to another cowboy and "swore off" cowpunching. In 1886 he thought he had made a sensible move. The day after he quit the LX he opened a small store—on a "six-bit scale"—in Caldwell.[6]

I   A Cowboy No More

There were several reasons why the life of a cowboy was no longer satisfactory for Siringo. He did not like being away from his wife for long periods of time, though he never became a stay-at-home. He had decided to write a book the winter before, hoping to make money from it. But, above all, he was discontented because of changes which were taking place. Perhaps his realization that the end of a great epoch had been reached prompted him both to write his book and to quit cowboying. He certainly thought things were not as they used to be. There was very little large-scale trail driving going on; the free range was rapidly disappearing; the "fool hoe-men" were taking the country. Where he had once helped to drive herds of 3,000, now he was driving only 800. Soon fences were to bring to an end nearly all trail driving, as well as other good aspects of the life he loved.

Siringo's A Texas Cow Boy, first published in 1885, was evidently written during Siringo's career as owner of a cigar and ice cream store in Caldwell. It is a lively lament for an age that was past, a monument, though perhaps not a monumental work, to the end of the open range. The 1885 edition, beautifully printed by M. Umbdenstock and Company of Chicago, is not the one referred to by Will Rogers as "the cowboy's Bible."[7] The book widely reprinted in paperback and sold by newsbutchers on the trains was the revised edition, printed in Chicago in 1886 by Siringo and Dobson; it contained a thirty-page section entitled "Addenda."

II A Texas Cow Boy, *1886*

It is unfortunate that the 1950 reprint of *A Texas Cow Boy*, edited by J. Frank Dobie, illustrated by Tom Lea, and published by William Sloane Associates, is of the 1885 instead of the 1886 edition. The Bison Book paperback, printed by the University of Nebraska Press in 1966 and reprinted in 1976, is a reprint of the Dobie edition. The first edition of a work is not always the best; one would not want to overlook, for instance, the wonderful chapter headings of later editions of Mark Twain's *Huckleberry Finn*. And I believe that the 1886 edition of *A Texas Cow Boy* is more representative of Siringo; the short "Addenda"section contains some of his most vivid writing.

On the surface, the postscript in the 1886 edition seems to be an effort at promoting emigration to the cattle ranges of the West, both of adventurous schoolboys and potential ranchmen. But when the time of composition is noted, February 1886, in the middle of the big storm of that year, which contributed about as much to the end of the open range as barbed wire did, it becomes evident that the entire essay is written with tongue in cheek and with some bitterness. Frequently, in the seemingly methodical account of how to get ahead in the West, Siringo's satire and biting humor emerge.

One must look at Siringo's vantage point in order to appreciate fully the irony of the situation. For fifteen years he had worked for wages, seeing the open range system develop from South Texas, the cradle of the Cattle Kingdom, and envelop the entire Great Plains area. He had seen the coming of barbed wire and the invasion of the "fool hoe man." At the time of the writing of the "Addenda" he could see the inevitable effects of the cold winter of 1885 - 1886. He saw the necessity of a new approach to cattle raising and probably deplored the necessity. Yet ostensibly the essay is a chamber of commerce prospectus containing advice on how to get rich quickly in an expanding cattle kingdom, written by an "old stove-up cow puncher," aged thirty-one, who had never been more than a cowboy with a maverick brand or, at best, a sort of straw boss moving small herds from the Texas Panhandle to Caldwell. His efforts at being a merchant, even "on a six-bit scale," were soon to fail, if

they had not already failed, and within two or three months he was
to become a Pinkerton detective—a "cowboy detective."

<h3 style="text-align:center">III   Advice to the Tenderfoot</h3>

The title of the new section of the 1886 edition reads as follows:

ADDENDA. THOSE WISHING INFORMATION AS TO PROFITS
AND LOSSES IN THE STOCK BUSINESS AS IT IS CARRIED ON AT
THE PRESENT DATE, CAN FIND IT—OR AT LEAST PART OF IT—
IN THE FOLLOWING PAGES; AND ALSO A FEW WORDS OF AD-
VICE TO THOSE WISHING TO SEEK WORK ON THE BROAD CAT-
TLE RANGES OF THE WEST.[8]

Obviously Siringo was not going to follow his own advice. A close
reading of the "Addenda" reveals his disillusion. He does not consistently adhere to the optimistic pattern of the usual emigrant
come-out literature. Truth breaks in and destroys the illusion he is
seeking to create. The tone of the introduction and the conclusion
of the original volume appears and reappears. As he did not permit
himself to be consistently romantic in his initial evaluation of the
Western cowboy experience, he could not take his advice to the
emigrant seriously.

In the first section Siringo sets the tone by describing how
maverickers in Texas "several years ago" were real humanitarians.
The mavericking outfits branded for themselves but also branded
their poor neighbors' mavericks—with the neighbors' brands, of
course—for 50 cents a head; these neighbors were widows or dis-
abled veterans—"crippled Rebels." The maverickers tallied these
brands with a forked pencil, that is, making two marks for every
maverick branded. But this was really a humanitarian move, Siringo
writes, for when the Eastern speculator—the "short horn"—entered
the cattle raising business with his eyes shut, he would buy entire
brands according to the "book count." Siringo writes,

Thus it will be seen that the forked pencil racket proved a blessing to the
poor. The day though, of inveigling the eastern tenderfoot into paying for
more than he really gets, is past, never more to return.[9]

Then Siringo outlines several ways of getting rich fast by raising
cattle on the "great cattle ranges of the west." He proves easily,
without his forked pencil, that $18 per steer was a sure potential

profit; that steers could be driven from South Texas, wintered, and sold for a profit of $9.75 a head; that one could start with 100 two-year-old heifers and amass a profit of $36,656 in ten years and still have 1,264 head of "she cattle" left for the future; and that one could, with a capital of $5,000, make a profit of $10,500 or more in ten years by raising horses.[10]

The economic possibilities, then, seemed to be marvelous indeed, but one does not even need to read between the lines. There is always a catch, and Siringo casually inserts his qualifying statements in the middle of his optimistic promotion of "the stock business of the great West." As he gives the cost of raising a three-year-old steer, as a sort of afterthought he remarks,

That is, at the present time. Of course as time glides on and the humane feeling which now exists in the east shall invade the west, then the cost will be more, as the building of sheds, etc., for winter use, will be necessary.[11]

After showing that the profit made on raising a yearling would be the same as that of raising a two-year-old, Siringo writes,

The only difference is, you have had the *fun* of putting in two years with the yearlings, which is quite an item, providing you don't value time nor money, and like the business.[12]

He advises newcomers to settle far away from the large Eastern syndicates, lest their calves become mavericks and be eaten or branded by the syndicate cowboys. Then he adds slyly that if the tenderfoot's conscience were like "your humble servant's," it would pay to settle *near* a large syndicate, because then the herd would increase faster and the entire operation could be sold "at good round figures" to the absentee owners.[13]

After showing the inevitability of the $36,656 profit Siringo concludes,

In estimating the above I have figured on your putting up a few stacks of prairie hay—although you might not need it often; when you did, it would be like the Texan's pistol, you would need it like - - - - -.[14]

In discussing the losses of a big cattle ranch, which he estimates at 3 percent, Siringo adds that this included losses from theft, since nowadays most people considered cattle stealing a crime. Then follows a paragraph that could well be the source of some of Charlie Russell's comments on the old-time cowboy:

82   CHARLES A. SIRINGO

Public opinion is causing lots of the old-time cowboys, or cow thieves, to
select other occupations; for, while they remain on the range, it is hard for
them to quit their old habits—which at one time were considered cute, as
well as legitimate. Those who are slow to take a tumble, are fast landing up
behind stone walls. The old-time cowboy will soon be like the buffalo and
mustang, a thing of the past; although we predict that the former can be
found in the city of Huntsville, in Texas, for a number of years to come. We
know of several young, healthy ones, friends of ours, who are now residing
there at the State's expense, and who are liable to live far into the next century, at which time the buffalo and mustang will have become extinct. [15]

But Siringo, himself an institution-free museum piece, advises the
would-be knight of the range on what kind of equipment he should
buy. He suggests that the style-minded neophyte could equip himself for $500, including $25 for a "spanish pony." On the other
hand, a utilitarian outfit, including the $25 pony, could be obtained
for $82. He suggests that a pistol, a $50 one or a $12 one, was an ab-
solute necessity:

If you are foolish enough to go without the latter, the cooks at the different
ranches where you happen to stop will not respect you. Instead of putting
the handle to your family name, they will call you the sorefooted kid, old
man Nibbs, or some such names as these. We know from experience that
the pistol carries much weight with it, and therefore especially advise the
young "tenderfoot" to buy one, even if he has to ride bare-backed, from
not having enough money left to buy a saddle with. [16]

Siringo's enthusiasm about the future of the greenhorn cowboy is
somewhat dampened as he complains that the life of the cowboy in
1886 required more "rough and tumble hard work than skill" and
that the cattle, bred up with shorthorns, were becoming so tame
that skill no longer was needed. He writes,

I believe the day is not far distant when cowboys will be armed with prod
poles—to punch the cattle out of the way—instead of fire-arms. Messrs.
Colt and Winchester will then have to go out of business, or else emigrate
to "Arkansaw" and open up prod-pole factories. [17]

Tongue in cheek, Siringo then points out that the cowboy could
soon be well off, since his expenses were very light—almost nothing
if he did not use tobacco, waste his time at gambling, or drink
whiskey. [18]

IV   *The Cow Pony*

One of the best written and most vivid sections of Siringo's "Addenda" is Part IV, entitled THE COW-PONY—AND HOW HE IS ABUSED ON THE LARGE CATTLE RANCHES.[19] After discussing the cowboy's "mount" of saddle horses, especially the "cutting" horses, Siringo describes the lot of a cow pony on a large ranch by showing in detail how "Curly," a summer cowboy from the East, abuses the pony. (Siringo suggests that the "dear reader" imagine himself in the horse's hide.) A day in the life of the horse is described in concrete detail. Beaten, abused, spurred till his sides are bloody, run until he is exhausted (part of the time chasing a coyote), the horse is turned loose without his back's being washed, with last year's saddle sores raw and bleeding. Siringo writes,

It is morning; and the sun is just peeping over yonder tree-tops, which are alive with little birds whose sweet melodious songs make the air ring with joy.

But there is no joy nor happiness for you. It is your day to be ridden, therefore you are roped and dragged up to where "Curly's" saddle lies. The bridle is put onto you, and then your lazy master picks up the dirty, hard, saddle blankets—which have not been washed for a month—and throws them over your raw and swollen back. Now for the saddle, which causes you to squirm and twist; and then to add to the pain, imagine a man whose weight, counting pistol, leggings and all, is one hundred and seventy-five pounds, climbing into the saddle.

You can now wake up, dear reader for we know you are disgusted playing the role of a sore-backed spanish cow pony.

But don't think for an instant that the majority of cow-boys are the cruel-hearted wretches, such as we have pictured this man "Curly" to be. There are though, on every range a few who can discount my friend Mr. "Curly" for cruelty.

Many a christian-hearted boy have I seen quit and throw up a paying job rather than ride one of those poor sore-backed brutes.

There should be a law passed in the west making it a penitentiary offense for an owner, or head man of a ranch to allow, or rather compel, a man to ride one of their sore-backed ponies, especially after the sore becomes so large that the saddle won't cover it, as is often the case.

V   *The End of an Era*

The last five paragraphs of Siringo's essay are filled with invective. The "old stove-up cow puncher" reveals his opinion of the way

the Range Cattle Industry had deteriorated. The strong indictment
of the get-rich-quick speculator, the Eastern absentee owner, is
impassioned:

We will mention the fact again that the free and easy day of successfully
raising stock in the wild and woolly west without winter feed, is past; and
thank the Lord it is! For it is cruel letting stock starve to death.

From where I sit while penning these lines, on this first day of February,
1886, I can look to the southward, into the Indian Territory, and see thousands of poor dumb brutes marching up and down those cursed barbed-
wire fences up to their knees in snow, with a blanket of ice an inch thick on
their backs, the piercing north wind blowing forty miles an hour, and not a
sprig of grass in sight.

Just think of it, ye cattle kings, while sitting in your city palaces roasting
your shins before a blazing fire! But methinks you will be reminded of the
fact next spring when you come out in your special car to attend the
general round-ups. Dead cattle scattered over the range don't look very
nice to the average eastern cattle king.

We think when you turn your faces towards the rising sun next fall you
will know that there has been lots of hay put up—especially those on the
Plains, or level ranges. From the present indications and reports, this winter
will cook the goose that has heretofore laid so many golden eggs. *Adios
Amegoes.*[20]

It is too bad that Siringo's reluctant recommendation of
rangeland resourcefulness, including the marvelously mixed
metaphor with which he ended his diatribe, has not been included
in modern reprints of *A Texas Cow Boy*. In the essay is some of
Siringo's best writing.

Siringo's prophecies in the "Addenda" came true. He quit the
cattle industry at a time when it was undergoing many vital
changes. He foresaw that the cowboy would gradually lose the indi-
viduality he possessed during the open range era and would acquire, more and more, the characteristics of an agricultural hired
hand. Ranching would become less haphazard—more scientific.

Despite his poking fun at cattlemen and cowboy life and despite his condemnation of the changing cattle kingdom, Siringo still
called himself a cowboy and did so for the rest of his life. Even
when he was a detective for the Pinkerton National Detective
Agency, he was the *cowboy* detective. He was interested in
anything pertaining to cowboy life, but always his interest lay in the

past, in the good old days when the West was uncrowded. Siringo
had a contempt for the modern cowboy. In 1927 he stated,

In late years a third crop of cowboys has sprung up to be trained for the
Wild West shows and the moving-picture studios.
There is very little need nowadays for the working cowboy, as the
Western cattle ranges are mostly fenced and the cattle so tame that one has
to shoo them out of the way to prevent being stepped on.[21]

Most of his writing was concerned with telling posterity of that
class of daredevil cowboys who paved the way for the "fool hoe-
men." The hoe-man, he says, will need no history, for he is here to
stay; when once a farmer gets his feet set on a piece of ground,
neither time nor cyclones can jar him loose. In 1927, when *Riata
and Spurs* was written, he hoped that a poem by Badger Clark, Jr.,
would be inscribed on his tombstone.

> 'Twas good to live when all the range
> Without no fence or fuss,
> Belonged in partnership with God,
> The Government and us.
>
> With skyline bounds from east to west,
> With room to go and come,
> I liked my fellow man the best
> When he was scattered some.
>
> When my old soul hunts range and rest
> Beyond the last divide,
> Just plant me on some strip of west
> That's sunny, lone and wide.
>
> Let cattle rub my headstone round,
> And coyotes wail their kin,
> Let hosses come and paw the mound,
> But don't you fence it in.[22]

CHAPTER 7

The Cowboy Detective

I *Siringo and Pinkerton's*

SIRINGO wrote the last lines of his "Addenda" to *A Texas Cow Boy* in February 1886, evidently at Caldwell, Kansas, where he had spent "two years and a half as a successful business man." This success, Siringo writes, "swelled his head" so that he thought he was "a natural born financier." He thought Caldwell was too small a town for a man of his ability; so he sold out and in the spring of 1886 he moved to Chicago, "a place more fitting for the expansion of [his] financial abilities." But, he writes, a few months in Chicago made it plain to him that his place was "in the saddle."[1]

It is probable that Siringo's statements about his financial success were as inflated as his description of how to get rich in the cattle industry; his success was more apparent than real. The photographs facing page 116 of *Riata and Spurs* show "Charlie Siringo's Store and Ice-Cream and Oyster Parlor in Caldwell" and a picture of "The Sign that Hung over the Bridge across Bluff Creek." This sign, an oil painting, shows "a mounted cowboy with a long-horn steer at the end of his rope." In the sky above the cowboy (the sign was oval-shaped) appears the advertisement: " 'Oklahoma Boomer' Cigars at Charlie Siringo's." The sign was "locked with iron chains" to the framework of the iron bridge. It was a favorite target of cowboys leaving Caldwell. Siringo says that the last time he saw it, "about twenty years later, it was riddled with bullet holes."[2]

Siringo "was there" when many of the great events of the settling of the West occurred. His store, which employed five clerks, capitalized on the unrest which preceded the big rush of 1889 when the Oklahoma Territory was opened for settlement. He says that he, in keeping with the times, became "the Oklahoma Border Cigar King," having put his special brand name, "The Oklahoma Boomer" on 100,000 cigars, which "sold like hot cakes."[3]

In May 1885 Siringo received publicity as a contestant in Caldwell's "grand cowboy tournament." First, he won a gold ring

86

for his sixteen-year-old wife, Mamie, by catching more rings on a long pole than any other contestant. It is interesting to find this contest, very popular in the postwar South and Southwest, in Caldwell. The bloodless tournament, a substitute for the bloodletting of the Age of Chivalry, consisted of a contest in which a rider, riding as fast as his horse would go, would attempt to catch on a lance a series of rings suspended from crossarms extending from posts. The tournament was accompanied by many of the traditions of the original tournament, with the contestants wearing their ladies' colors and presenting them with the prizes. Siringo also won a silver cup in a steer-roping contest. The "grand cowboy tournament" seems to have included at least some of the contests of the modern rodeo.[4]

I doubt that Siringo's move to Chicago in 1886 was entirely a result of ambition. A cigar, ice cream, and oyster parlor in Caldwell, Kansas, in 1886 would be unlikely to draw customers as successfully as would a saloon. But Siringo had tasted city life and ways. A Chicago publisher, M. Umbdenstock and Company, in all likelihood merely a printing company, had published *A Texas Cow Boy*, a second edition of which was evidently in the making; Siringo and Dobson published it in 1886. It is probable that the book and its promotion took him to Chicago. At any rate, Chicago was the headquarters of the Pinkerton's National Detective Agency, for which Siringo was the "cowboy" detective for twenty years.

The experiences of these years are related in four of Siringo's books: *A Cowboy Detective* (1912), *Two Evil Isms: Pinkertonism and Anarchism* (1915), *Riata and Spurs* (first edition, 1927), and *A Lone Star Cowboy* (1919). The account in *A Lone Star Cowboy* is very brief.

A comparison of these four works is revealing of the difficulties Siringo had with Pinkerton's. *A Cowboy Detective* was published in 1912 in Chicago by W. B. Conkey. As Charles D. Peavy indicates, a Chicago court enjoined Siringo from revealing information about Pinkerton's operations and from using the original title, "Pinkerton's Cowboy Detective, A True Story of Twenty-two Years with Pinkerton's National Detective Agency." The court decree is very explicit about both matters. In his account of the matter in his report to Houghton Mifflin Company when the publication of *Riata and Spurs* was being considered, Siringo emphasized the change of names in the book, but the lawyer representing Pinkerton's emphasized the content of Siringo's account, indicating disapproval of the book's revealing Pinkerton's secrets.[5]

In the book as finally published, *A Cowboy Detective*, the subtitle on the title page is *A True Story of Twenty-Two Years with a World-Famous Detective Agency*: the subtitle on the cover is *An Autobiography*. In the book itself "Pinkerton" becomes "Dickinson," and other names are thinly disguised. The book is illustrated, incidentally, with photographs; the identity of the characters involved could not be disguised. Basically, the censorship was ineffective.

In his preface to *A Cowboy Detective* Siringo writes,

This story. . .has been delayed for a long time in coming from the press. The delay was due to the protests of the author's former employers. These protests were undoubtedly rightful, but it was considered in the beginning that no harm could come therefrom, for the reason that the identity of the persons involved was not disclosed except in reference to past facts, matters that were done and over with. Now this difficulty has been overcome and the objections removed by the use of fictitious names in many places.[6]

Siringo's assumption was that the changing of the names satisfied the detective agency in 1912, in spite of the fact that identifications could be readily made. However, later Pinkerton's did not accept his assumption. An examination of *A Cowboy Detective* seems to justify Siringo's assumption. It was well known, for instance, that Pinkerton detectives were involved in the Coeur d'Alene, Idaho, strikes of 1892, which Siringo describes in detail. The superintendent of Pinkerton's National Detective Agency at Denver, James McParland, is called James McCartney. In *A Cowboy Detective* the chapter heading for Chapter XXI lists McParland by his real name, both in the text and in the Table of Contents. Also, the picture of "Jas. McCartney and the Author," facing page 514, was from the Pinkerton files and was later reproduced in one of the books written with the cooperation of the agency.[7] Tom Horn, one of the more infamous Pinkerton detectives, appears as Tim Corn, even on the caption of his picture. The people in the book are so easily identified that Pinkerton's attempt to obscure the fact that Siringo was writing about his life as a Pinkerton detective seems paranoid, especially when the agency achieved the censorship of *Riata and Spurs*.

Two Evil Isms: Pinkertonism and Anarchism was obviously a result of Siringo's resentment at being censored. Although the book is brief, containing only 109 pages, in contrast to the 519 pages of *A Cowboy Detective*, it does give the real names of the people involved. Although *Two Evil Isms* was printed, Pinkerton's took the matter to court, located the plates and unsold copies of the book, and gained possession of them. Sufficient copies of the book, however, were distributed for the work to be available to scholars. The story of Siringo's experience with the publication of *Two Evil Isms* is told in Charles D. Peavy's introduction to the 1967 reprint of the book. In Siringo's report to Houghton Mifflin Company on the publication history of *A Cowboy Detective* he states that later (after the settlement of the publication problems of the detective book) he did something to William A. Pinkerton to incur his lifelong enmity. It may be safely assumed, I believe, that Siringo was referring to the publication of *Two Evil Isms*.[8]

A Lone Star Cowboy, printed in Santa Fe in 1919, gives the real names of those involved in Siringo's work as a detective, but fewer than sixty pages deal with Siringo's life as a detective. Evidently Pinkerton's thought the book beneath their notice, and maybe it was. The other books about the agency were printed in Chicago, right under the corporate nose. When Siringo again published a book which named names and cited specific cases, this time with a nationally known publisher, Pinkerton's National Detective Agency again exerted its power.

II Riata and Spurs

The publication history of *Riata and Spurs* reflects the power of Pinkerton's in suppressing publication of materials which involved the agency. Correspondence and interoffice memoranda involving Siringo are in the Houghton Mifflin archives in the Houghton Library of Harvard University.

A memorandum early in 1926 indicates that Houghton Mifflin was considering publishing or reprinting several of Siringo's works. *The Song Companion to A Lone Star Cowboy* was dismissed as being inconsequential. *History of "Billy the Kid"* was also not considered because the information it contains is found elsewhere in Siringo's books. *A Cowboy Detective* and *A Lone Star Cowboy* were cited as having the best possibilities, although the suggestion was made that both needed to be toned down for publication by Houghton Mifflin. The unpublished manuscript "The Bad Men Cowboys" was thought to be the least publishable of the works being considered.[9]

One might assume that *Riata and Spurs,* which combined information from *A Lone Star Cowboy* and *A Cowboy Detective,* was a result of Houghton Mifflin's evaluation of the first two books if it were not for the fact that a memorandum dated less than two months later indicated that publication of *Riata and Spurs* was already being planned. A memorandum written about ten days later indicated that the detective material had not yet been received and that much editing would be done by the publisher. A memorandum written about a month later indicated that the manuscript was not complete and that the material Siringo had already sent would be returned to him so that he would know what needed to be done. A later memorandum indicated that the manuscript "The Bad Men Cowboys" would not be considered for publication until *Riata and Spurs*, a composite manuscript, was completed. Later memoranda concern Gifford Pinchot's writing an introduction to *Riata and Spurs* and the photographs which would illustrate the book.[10]

In a memorandum dated January 18, 1927, to which an undated statement from Siringo about the publication history of *A Cowboy Detective* was attached, the question of the mention of Pinkerton's National Detective Agency was raised; it was assumed that the agency would have no objection to the book. Siringo's statement was that Pinkerton's objection to *A Cowboy Detective* was only to the use of the name of the agency, although the original injunction plainly states that Siringo was not to reveal through publication any information or knowledge which he had acquired while an employee of the agency.[11] Siringo's belief that the injunction had applied only to the use of the agency's name and the names of individuals is understandable: *A Cowboy Detective* had been published without change except for name changes.

At any rate, according to the publisher's files, *Riata and Spurs* was published on April 22, 1927, and almost 5,000 copies were sold. But, as the files show, all was not well.[12]

On May 27, 1927, the lawyer who represented the detective agency wrote a long letter to the Chicago office of Houghton Mifflin Company, reviewing accurately the legal history of the publication of *A Cowboy Detective* and *Two Evil Isms*. He included a copy of the original injunction. He called *Riata and Spurs* a book about "a so-called cowboy detective" and said that after the publication of *Two Evil Isms* Siringo was indicted for criminal libel but that the governor of New Mexico refused extradition. The letter insisted that publication of the detective material was in violation of the injunction and had to be stopped; the items involving Pinkerton's had to be suppressed. The detective agency did not move from this stand throughout the controversy.

On May 31, 1927, the Chicago office of Houghton Mifflin sent a telegram to Boston stating that the Pinkerton agency had threatened to get an injunction and to sue for damages if the Siringo book were continued in publication; the Chicago office also asked for full information. The Boston office replied the same day, pointing out that Pinkerton's had not objected to the publication of *A Cowboy Detective* with the names changed and that in 1914 the book had been reprinted using the agency's name in the text and on the cover, without any objection from Pinkerton's. (Siringo's statement mentions only that Pinkerton's name was used on the cover of the 1914 edition.) The telegram states that Siringo believed that no legal objection remained and that the case ought to be dropped "on the grounds of common sense."

On June 21, 1927, the Pinkerton lawyer wired the Boston office of Houghton Mifflin stating that *Riata and Spurs* was in violation of the Chicago injunction and demanding that all publication and sale of the book cease. If Pinkerton's demand was not agreed to, the telegram stated, steps would be taken to enforce the injunction. A handwritten note, dated June 21, indicates that copies of *Riata and Spurs* were being folded. The printers were instructed to complete the folding but to do nothing further until they received instructions.

A telegram from the agency's lawyer to the Boston office of Houghton Mifflin, dated June 23, 1927, suggested that one of the publisher's officials confer in New York with the agency and stated that if an agreement could not be reached, the agency would go to court. Evidently this meeting was held, because a curt, three-sentence letter dated June 27, 1927, from the general manager of Pinkerton's New York office stated that a letter left with the New York office was being returned. The letter evidently was Siringo's evaluation of the case, mentioned earlier. The manager of the New York office stated that "this party" Siringo was "totally unreliable in every particular." Thus Siringo's account of the publication of *A Cowboy Detective* was labeled as containing no truth, although in fact it was *almost* accurate, and Siringo himself was branded as a liar.

On June 30, 1927, a letter from Houghton Mifflin to the New York office of Pinkerton's indicated that an attempt was being made to salvage a part of *Riata and Spurs*. After extolling Pinkerton's for its achievements in law enforcement, the letter suggested that certain well-known events be retained in the book, even though they did involve the detective agency. On July 12, 1927, a memorandum from the New York office of Houghton Mifflin states that the general manager of the New York office of Pinkerton's had asked Allen Pinkerton about the matter and would reply soon. On July 13, 1927, the New York office of the publisher sent a memorandum to the Boston office stating that the Pinkerton's New York general manager had called, stating that Pinkerton's expected Houghton Mifflin to "live up to the letter of the injunction which they obtained." That did it.

On the same day, July 13, 1927, Siringo was informed of the company's decision to censor *Riata and Spurs*, with a reference being made to the old injunction. On July 15, 1927, a letter was written to Siringo saying that Pinkerton's had threatened to sue if the book was continued in circulation and stating that Houghton Mifflin had believed Siringo's statement that there was no obstacle to publication of the Pinkerton material. It was suggested that material from "Flashes from a Cowboy Pen," which Siringo had submitted the previous winter, and from "The Bad Men Cowboys" be substituted for the detective material.

Siringo, on July 19, 1927, suggested that the names in *Riata and Spurs* be changed, as had been done in *A Cowboy Detective*. If this were not possible, Siringo agreed that material from the other manuscipts be substituted. The next day, July 20, 1927, he wrote again, reiterating his belief that the last part of *Riata and Spurs* could be salvaged by giving fictional names to the people involved, as he had done in *A Cowboy Detective*. He (rightly) doubted the wisdom of using "The Bad Men Cowboys" manuscript, since that material was not from his own experience, and suggested as an alternative the use of *A Texas Cow Boy* and the enlargement of the Billy the Kid episode.

But on July 21, 1927, Houghton Mifflin informed the New York office of Pinkerton's of the proposed changes. A copy of the book with the changes indicated was being sent the agency, and the letter stated that the substituted material would be sent to Pinkerton's for approval. On the same day a telegram was sent to Siringo telling him of the proposed changes; the omitted material would be replaced by material from "The Bad Men Cowboys."

Giving up completely, Siringo on July 21, 1927, in a telegram to

Houghton Mifflin, approved of the changes. In a letter written the next day, July 22, 1927, he made suggestions as to how further changes could be made to satisfy the agency. A letter from the New York general manager of Pinkerton's, same date, to Houghton Mifflin very briefly stated that the agency would wait and see what the revised book looked like.

Then on July 26, 1927, an editor other than the one who had been working with Siringo wrote Siringo explaining the changes which had been made in *Riata and Spurs*. Siringo replied on August 12, 1927, suggesting other changes. On August 12, 1927, he was sent galley proofs of the revision; although he was not asked to proofread the galleys he did proofread them, correcting some errors, as indicated in his letter of August 16, 1927. He also commented that the bookstores in California had already raised the price of the original book because of the revision. On August 17, 1927, Siringo made another suggestion of a change in a photograph caption which had originally appeared in the detective section, so as not to offend Pinkerton's. In his final letter to Houghton Mifflin, dated August 25, 1927, he suggested similar minor changes. Old and ill, Siringo had given up.

When one considers the power that the Pinkerton National Detective Agency still exercised as late as 1927, it is not surprising that Houghton Mifflin gave in to the agency's demands. Pinkerton's, especially the New York general manager, was firm and unrelenting. It now appears that the publisher could have won if Pinkerton's had chosen to sue, on the grounds that no exception had been taken to the publication of the revised *A Cowboy Detective*. It is possible, however, that Siringo might have been subjected to further harassment by Pinkerton's if Houghton Mifflin had resisted. At any rate the story is a revealing one. One sympathizes with the publisher; the Pinkerton communications reveal an implacable adversary.

Siringo seemed to recognize that the agency's reaction to *Two Evil Isms* and its suppression had something to do with the suppression of the Pinkerton material in *Riata and Spurs*. He had not been forgiven by William A. Pinkerton for the publication of *Two Evil Isms*, a good many copies of which had been distributed. And, after all, the Pinkerton victories came too late to prevent distribution of either book. Thousands of copies of the original *Riata and Spurs* were sold, and sufficient copies of *Two Evil Isms* escaped suppression for it to be readily available, at least in libraries. The reprinting of *Two Evil Isms* was evidently done without difficulty, and the time is right for the reprinting of the other Siringo books.

Especially now there should be no problem in publishing a revised edition of *A Cowboy Detective*, with Siringo's original identifications restored, or reprinting the first edition of *Riata and Spurs*. In the 1940s the Pinkerton National Detective Agency opened its files to James D. Horan, who has written at least two books from the files.[13] Siringo appears, though briefly, in both books, and no comment is made as to the accuracy of his accounts.

III   *The True Account*

Siringo's purpose in writing *A Texas Cow Boy* was in part to correct the inaccuracies of the dime novels. The same purpose is given for the writing of *A Cowboy Detective;* in his preface Siringo writes,

The author is not a literary man, but has written as he speaks, and it is thought that the simplicity thus resulting will not detract from the substantial merit of the tales, which are recitals of facts and not fiction.[14]

But Siringo was hampered in his attempt to present his "recital of facts" about his experiences as a detective by the Pinkerton Agency's persistent effort to maintain the secrecy of its operations. The agency succeeded in harassing Siringo and driving him to making threats of publishing his account in "a new book for an Eastern publisher" or of publishing *Two Evil Isms* with the support of the National Socialist party.[15]

As usual, Pinkerton's won, but, as has been shown, the victory was an empty one. Anyone can correlate the three books, extracting the events from *A Cowboy Detective* and the names from *Two Evil Isms* and *Riata and Spurs*, and thus arrive at Siringo's facts. A study of these three basic volumes will help one to understand the actions of Charlie Siringo, the cowboy detective.

IV   *Phrenology and the Future*

As was his wont, Siringo felt obliged to justify his becoming a detective for the Pinkerton's National Detective Agency. The truth was, he writes, that in 1884, before he left Caldwell, Kansas, a blind phrenologist came to Caldwell and gave a lecture at the Leland

Hotel. First the blind man felt of the head of Henry Brown, the town marshal who had been a member of Billy the Kid's gang; Theodore Baufman, the Oklahoma Indian Scout; and Mamie, Siringo's sixteen-year-old wife. According to Siringo, who knew all three people well, the analyses were accurate. Neither Brown, who later was killed after he robbed a bank, nor Baufman, whose laziness and skill at lying were pointed out, liked what the old man said. And, Siringo writes, the crowd knew that the good things he said about Mamie were true.

The crowd shouted for the phrenologist to analyze Siringo, who did not seem to mind being in the limelight. First, the blind man, laying his hand on the top of Siringo's head, said, "Ladies and gentlemen, here is a mule's head." After the laughter died down, the old man explained that Siringo's bump of stubbornness was large— he was stubborn as a mule. Then he said that Siringo "had a fine head for a newspaper editor, a fine stock raiser, or a detective." He would be a success in any of these professions.[16]

So when Siringo arrived in Chicago in the spring of 1886 he was looking for financial opportunities and a chance to see the world. He and Mamie were living on Harrison Avenue on the night of the Haymarket riot, May 4, when a bomb was thrown in the middle of a squad of police officers. During the excitement of the riot Siringo, who had had experience as a range detective, wished he were a detective "so as to help ferret out the thrower of the bomb and his backers."

So, with a letter of recommendation from a local bank, S.A. Kean and Company, Siringo went to the Pinkerton Detective Agency, where he was interviewed by William A. Pinkerton, and gave banker David T. Beals, Sheriff James H. East, and Pat Garrett as references. Eventually Siringo was hired by the agency, but not before he spent some time in jail for fighting in the streets.[17] His first assignment was in the Haymarket riot case.

CHAPTER 8

The Anarchists

A CCORDING to bitter retrospect, as revealed in *Two Evil Isms*, Siringo saw at once that the Pinkerton National Detective Agency, "that model institution" engaged in "a righteous cause," was a "school for the making of anarchists." Although he had hoped "to help stamp out this great Anarchist curse [bombings such as that in the Haymarket case]," he soon came to believe that the Pinkerton operatives were worse than the anarchists themselves. He was especially incensed about operatives' mainly false reports about Albert Parsons, one of the accused men, made for the purpose of pleasing the clients and the agency, building up the reputation of the detective, and the running up of large expense accounts.[1]

Why, then, did not Siringo immediately quit the agency, instead of working for it for the next twenty-two years? Well, no one has ever accused Siringo of being a great thinker or even a man strong on principle. His thinking was uncomplicated. He was, like the average American of his time, against the "foreign-born anarchists" who were upsetting the status quo. He saw the corruption within the agency but felt that he could work within the agency and still help to keep down anarchy, that disturbingly destructive force in American society. The fact that sometimes his own methods were morally questionable did not matter. In his simplistic thinking, the end, that of restoring law and order, justified the means. He was in step with the times—an age which could convict the "Haymarket anarchists" on the basis that they were anarchists and not on evidence that they were involved in the bombing. About his decision to stay with Pinkerton's Siringo wrote,

The lessons of injustice learned during my first month in the big agency almost caused me to throw up my position in disgust. But I argued in my own mind that the corruption was a sore on the body politic, which no one man could cure—hence, I might as well remain and become educated into the ways of free America, where all men and women are considered kings and queens, and the children kinglets and queenlets.

The question might be asked why I did not show my manhood by resign-
ing and exposing this crooked agency in the beginning. Exposing it to
whom, pray? Not to the officers of the law, I hope. In my cowboy simplicity
I might have been persuaded to do so at that time. But I am glad I did not,
for, with my twenty-two years behind the curtains, I can now see the outcome. It would have resulted in many "sleeps" in the city bull-pen, and a
few doses of the "third degree" to try and wring a confession for blackmail-
ing this notorious institution. . . .

A man without wealth and influence trying to expose the dastardly work
of the Pinkerton National Detective Agency would be like a two-year-old
boy blowing his breath against a cyclone to stop its force. . . .[2]

It is easy to understand Siringo's viewpoint. Basically he was a
law-and-order man. In the agency he could, as a cowboy detective,
chase outlaws in the West—and he did. But he could also pursue
anarchists, mainly those who were involved in the labor movement
in the West, among the hardrock miners.

I   The Age of Violence: Anarchy

In many ways the thirty-five years between the end of the Civil
War and the turn of the century were remarkable years. They saw
the rise, development, and end of the Range Cattle Industry, the
result of the killing of the buffalo herds and the subjugation of the
Plains Indians. Immigration, especially from Europe, was heavy.
With the development of large manufacturing plants, America
became a leading industrial, capitalistic nation. In part a result, at
least a psychological result, of the end of the frontier, which
Frederick Jackson Turner dated as 1890, labor unions developed in
America on a national scale. Labor riots and race riots were common. Periodically outlaw gangs thrived. Slavery in the South eventually was supplanted by the tenant farm system and Jim Crow
laws. Pinkerton's Detective Agency grew as the nation spread
geographically and as violence became more common.

Siringo did not "go west and grow up with the country." He was
already there, and he witnessed more than his share of the violent
events. His first assignment with Pinkerton's placed him in the middle of the Haymarket Affair.[3]

II   The Haymarket Affair

The Haymarket Affair was the result of a meeting of "lumber

shovers'' who were on strike for shorter hours at the McCormick
reaper works in Chicago. There was a picket line at the plant, a
result of a shut-out.

August Spies, one of the defendants in the Haymarket trial, had
addressed the meeting. During the address, workers left the McCormick Plant, and about five hundred of the locked-out unionists attacked the nonunion workers. Police and riot squads entered the
fray, killing two unionists and wounding many others. The meeting
at Haymarket Square was for the purpose of protesting police
brutality at the other meeting.

On May 4, 1886, at about 8:30, Spies began a rather mild speech
of about twenty minutes. Then Albert Parsons arrived and began a
rather calm forty-five-minute speech. Mayor Harrison, whose police
were ready for a riot, mingled with the crowd, and, thinking the
audience was orderly, ordered the police chief and the reserves to
go home.

At about ten o'clock Samuel Fielden began to speak. Scouts from
the police station reported to Inspector "Black Jack" Bonfield that
Fielden's comments attacked the law. He ordered a company of 176
men to march on the meeting.

Captain Word of the police demanded that the meeting "immediately and peaceably disperse." Fielden, Spies, and Parsons began
to descend from the wagon which had served as a platform, with
Fielden assuring the police that the meeting was peaceable. At that
moment a bomb was thrown near the front ranks of the police company; it exploded immediately. Inspector Bonfield ordered the
police to fire, which they did, in all directions.

Both Fielden and Spies were wounded, as were many others.
Seven policemen were killed and sixty-seven others wounded, some
from the bomb and others by bullets. In the confusion, some
thought, policemen had wounded each other.[4]

Siringo heard the explosion of the bomb; a young lawyer, whose
room was next to Siringo's, wanted Siringo to go with him to the
riot, but Mamie, Siringo says, would not let Charlie get out of bed.
But Siringo lent Reynolds his "silver-plated, pearl-handled Colt's.45
pistol," which Reynolds returned about thirty minutes later.
Policemen, evidently thinking Reynolds was one of the anarchists,
had fired on him; so he quickly returned home.[5]

Siringo's first assignment for Pinkerton's was, he says, to visit the

German saloon where the anarchists spent their evenings. When the trials started, he was detailed to watch the jury so that lawyers for the defense could not bribe them. In *Two Evil Isms* Siringo says he was told that the jury had already been "fixed" by the prosecution.

Those whom the officers had arrested and were in the courtroom were Louis Lingg, August Spies, George Engel, Michael Schwab, Oscar Neebe, Adolph Fischer, and Samuel Fielden. As the court opened, Albert Parsons walked in and took his place with the other seven prisoners. "Little did he dream," Siringo writes in *Two Evil Isms*, "that he was running his head into a noose manufactured by the Pinkerton National Detective Agency."[6.]

Siringo thus heard most of the testimony. He thought, especially, that the evidence against Neebe was weak. In *Two Evil Isms* he states that no doubt some of the anarchists deserved hanging, but as he understood the evidence, there was no justice in the conviction.

He states that a Pinkerton operative told him that an anarchist named Schnaubelt, who supposedly threw the bomb, was murdered while being given the third degree by police. This story has been shown to be false; it is possible that Siringo's information about the Pinkerton Agency's fabrication of evidence may have been false also.[7]

At any rate, all of the eight "anarchists" were judged guilty. Parsons, Engel, Fischer, and Spies were hanged (and immediately were declared martyrs), Lingg "blew his head off in jail with a bomb" before he was executed, and Schwab and Fielden received life sentences and Neebe a lesser sentence.[8] On June 26, 1893, Governor John P. Altgelt of Illinois pardoned Schwab, Fielden, and Neebe, on the grounds that the evidence did not show them guilty and that "the judge conducted the trial with malicious ferocity." He believed at the time, rightly, that his political career had been destroyed by the pardons.[9]

Siringo's early conclusions about the Haymarket Affair differed somewhat from his later opinions. In about 1910, in *A Cowboy Detective* (1912), he wrote,

A million dollars had been subscribed by the Citizens' League to stamp out anarchy in Chicago, and no doubt much of it was used to corrupt justice. Still, the hanging of these anarchists had a good effect and was worth a million dollars to society. Now, if the law-abiding people of the whole Un-

ited States would contribute one hundred times one million dollars to
stamp out anarchy and dynamiting, the coming generation would be saved
much suffering and bloodshed, for we are surely playing with fire when we
receive with open arms anarchists from foreign countries and pat them on
the back for blowing up Russian and English royalty. These chickens will
come home to roost in our back yard some day.[10]

Siringo neither studiously avoided the cliche nor eschewed the
mixed metaphor. Too, as we have seen, his evaluations in 1910 differed from those in *Two Evil Isms*. Siringo was against anarchy; to
him this anarchy was brought in by foreigners (though Albert Parsons's ancestors were in America before the American Revolution[11]).
Also, both of Siringo's parents were immigrants, his father from
Italy and his mother from Ireland.

Ironically, Siringo's second important assignment, while he was
still in Chicago, was "against the Irish National League, for the
English government." He says that the Irish League consisted of
"would-be destroyers of the English crown."[12] The Siringos were
happy when he was transferred to the Denver office, in the fall of
1886.[13]

III   *Anarchy in Colorado*

Throughout his life Siringo looked on himself as a cowboy. A part
of his dissatisfaction with his work in Chicago was that he could not
do it on horseback. He was the cowboy detective; his initial agreement with William A. Pinkerton was that he eventually would work
as a cowboy detective out of the Denver office. One of his favorite
photographs shows him trailing train robbers. He is dressed in
rough cowboy clothes, mounted on a large horse, and leading a
pack horse on which are packed a bedroll, cooking utensils, etc.[14]
He seemed to be able to ride long distances over rough territory in
the worst kind of weather in pursuit of the Western outlaw—and
even take delight in the pursuit—just as he received a "glow and a
glee" from following the longhorn steer.

In early spring 1887 Siringo set out on his first "cowboy operation," a political dispute in Archuleta County, in Southwest
Colorado on the New Mexico border.[15] Siringo writes, "By the
newspapers it was called an uprising of anarchists, but in truth it
was anarchy against anarchy, with the school of anarchy, my
agency, as a third party."[16]

Siringo's analysis seems accurate. The forces in conflict were "American" residents against "Mexican" sheep ranchers, election by fraud and rebellion of the defeated, insurgents against duly elected (though fradulently elected) officials.

Government on the American frontier, where the population was scattered, was at best difficult. The Archuleta County difficulty was not unique. Similar conflicts existed throughout the West. During the same period, Hidalgo County, Texas, experienced conflicts similar to those in Colorado, although the Texas problems seem to have lasted longer (1876 to 1895, at least), possibly because the Rio Grande Valley of Texas was a more isolated frontier. There Siringo's "anarchy" was frequently present, with the duly (fraudulently?) elected officials frequently being driven across the Rio Grande.[17]

Archuleta County is the third county west of the southwest corner of Colorado. Its situation on the border of the New Mexico territory (the nearest railroad was at Amargo, New Mexico Territory) made election fraud possible. The uprising, called anarchy by the Denver newspapers, was the result, according to Siringo, of the Archuleta brothers, of Amargo, ruling politically by importing to the county on election day their New Mexican sheep herders to vote in Colorado.

The citizens of Archuleta County (evidently the Archuletas owned land in both Colorado and New Mexico Territory) finally rebelled and drove all the county officers except the sheriff and county clerk out of the county, into New Mexico. The sheriff and county clerk were "Americans," while only one of the county commissioners (he had a Mexican wife) and the county attorney were Anglos. Three of the four Mexican-American county commissioners were named Archuleta.

Siringo's method of operation in the Archuleta County uprising is typical of his cowboy detective approach. The detective agency was employed by the deposed officials, who, in order to retain their offices, had to hold a county commissioners' meeting within sixty days after election. The problem was simple; the insurgent group (Siringo calls them "revolutionists") was determined not to permit the elected officials to return to the county. Siringo's assignment was twofold: to help the elected officials hold the meeting and to accumulate evidence against the insurgents.

Siringo's approach was to become one of the revolutionists and to work from within the group. So, using the alias Anderson, he went by train to Durango, Colorado, where he bought a horse and saddle and rode the sixty miles to Pagosa Springs, the county seat of Archuleta County. On the way he stopped at the ranch of "one of the ringleaders of the uprising," who was supposed to be a bad man from Texas.

Siringo made himself solid with the rancher by confiding how he had killed three Mexicans in Texas and had left hurriedly. The rancher was a fugitive from Texas.

When he arrived at Pagosa Springs Siringo gained the confidence of the county clerk, who was the leader of the revolutionaries, by presenting himself as a friend of the rancher. Siringo told of his being a fugitive from Texas—he capitalized on his outlawry throughout the assignment—and the county clerk, after getting the consent of his wife (Siringo says he took long enough to get the consent of ten men), invited Siringo to live with them. Siringo writes, "Mrs. Taylor was a splendid cook, and the warm supper hit the soft spot in my heart. And the nice clean bed in a cozy front room put me at peace with the world."[18]

Soon after Siringo arrived at Pagosa Springs, the county commissioners, County Judge J. Archuleta, and the county attorney attempted to enter the town with an armed escort of sixty Mexicans, in order to hold their meeting. The seventy-five revolutionists, mostly wild and woolly cowboys and ranchmen, Siringo among them, met the officials at the San Juan River bridge and turned them back. Communication was made under flags of truce.

So the county officials drew back and camped in an old house on the south side of the river, with the armed escort being housed in a nearby abandoned government barracks.

The subversives plotted to kill the officials at three o'clock the next morning. The plan was to set fire to a haystack near the old house and to assassinate the officials as they left the burning building. Siringo waded the river and warned the guards about the plan; the leader of the guards was supposed to give Siringo time to get back to town before he notified the county officials, but he did not wait. Siringo immediately was suspected and escaped hanging only because the county clerk, the sheriff, and his rancher friend believed in his innocence and because Siringo's clothing, which he had removed while crossing the river, was dry.

So those insurgents who remained suspicious believed that Siringo had given the plot away to the Mexican wife of the Anglo commissioner; she had been permitted to live in a shack on the bank of the river. A guard was placed on the shack in an effort to catch Siringo, who went to the shack to leave some shorthand notes in the back of an old oil painting. He passed only a few yards from the woodpile where the armed guard was hiding. After leaving his notes, he talked briefly to the woman, then left the shack by slipping a board out of place in the back wall and jumping several feet to the rocky edge of the river.

In the meantime the insurgents, who had been at a dance, were told that Siringo was in the shack. Heavily armed, they descended on the shack but found no one there except the woman and her children. She was adamant, insisting that Siringo had not been there. When Siringo returned to town, no men were in the dance hall except the two fiddlers.

When the mob of armed men returned, Siringo's rancher friend took him aside and questioned him. Siringo's first impulse was to fight his way out of the trap, but he thought that would be showing bad detective ability. When Siringo's friend asked him point-blank whether he was a detective, Siringo said no and even denied that he had been in the woman's shack. When he was told that one of the insurgents had seen him go into the shack, Siringo loudly demanded to be shown "the dirty whelp that would tell such a lie" on him, threatening to kill the man. The confrontation took place, the man admitted that he could have made a mistake, and Siringo was safe for the time being.

The next day, when the mob again became aroused, Siringo did some imaginative lying and not only convinced the mob but was appointed as special sheriff's deputy at $4 per day. This money, Siringo says, was "all velvet," an extra bonus.

Two days later Siringo prevented the murder of the officials by warning one of them when the insurgents planned to slaughter the county officials after both sides supposedly had stacked their arms in one place. Finally, after about four days, peace was declared, with the commissioners holding their meeting after the revolutionists were promised an even division of the political spoil in the future. After the meeting the commissioners returned to New Mexico. Siringo writes, "The blood of the insurgents had cooled off as the liquors in Bowland's saloon diminished, hence peace was declared under a flag of truce—a woman's white apron." [19]

For the next six weeks detective - deputy sheriff Siringo played outlaw, ate Mrs. Taylor's good cooking, and hid out when suspicious strangers came to Pagosa Springs and the sheriff warned him. During the county clerk's absence, he read the man's private political letters and examined his receipts for votes bought during past elections. The going price for a vote was two dollars or one sheep. From these records, Siringo says, he "learned many new lessons in up-to-date western politics." At the end of the period, Siringo appeared before a grand jury at Durango; sixteen of the insurgents were indicted. Siringo sold his horse and saddle and sneaked aboard a train bound east for Denver.

Later Siringo wrote the county clerk from Mexico, where he was working on another case. The insurgents suspected that Siringo had betrayed them to the grand jury and were ready to hang him, but the county clerk and his wife defended Siringo to the last and assured him that he would always have friends in Pagosa Springs. At the time of the writing of A *Cowboy Detective* the former county clerk was a judge in Pagosa Springs.

It is interesting to speculate about whether the insurgents ever read Siringo's book.

IV   *Coeur d'Alene*

The period of Siringo's work as Pinkerton's cowboy detective was one of violence among the hard-rock miners of the West. It was during this time that Big Bill Haywood, president of the Western Federation of Miners and eventually one of the organizers of the International Workmen of the World, was active. Violence was common, and dynamite was a favorite weapon. Labor unions seem to have gone further than they should have, in that an attempt was made to close down operation of the mines. The intemperate violence of the unions has been described frequently by those sympathetic with the mine owners, but it is probable that the mine owners had a better press. It is also probable that the violence of the strikes was excessive.

Siringo, as a Pinkerton operative, was directly involved in one of the most famous of the labor riots of the 1890s, the trouble in the Coeur d'Alene district in the Idaho Panhandle in 1891 and 1892. It is probable that Siringo's books have done much to publicize the Coeur d'Alene troubles. His account, especially that in A *Cowboy Detective*, is detailed, even exciting, and Siringo obviously is the hero. Mary Hallock Foote's novel, a part of which is based on Siringo's testimony at the trial, is pallid when contrasted with

Siringo's story, as one would expect, and the accounts of the strike by John Hays Hammond and William T. Stoll are matter-of-fact, although in detail they corroborate Siringo's story.[20] Hammond and Stoll were mine owners.

In the fall of 1891 Superintendent James McParland told Siringo to get ready for a long assignment in the Coeur d'Alene mining country. When he was told that his job would include joining the union and reporting their secrets to the mine owners, Siringo says he refused because he sympathized with the laborers and was opposed to the capitalists.

About a month later McParland called Siringo in and, according to Siringo, said,

"Now, Charlie, you have got to go to the Coeur d'Alenes. You are the only man I have got who can do the work right. The other operative I sent there was suspected and had to skip out to save his life. I am going to make you a proposition: You go there and join the union. If you find the miners are in the right and the mine owners wrong, come home at once; otherwise stay to the finish."

Siringo agreed to what seemed to him to be a fair proposal.[21] After being in Idaho for a month or two, Siringo says, his sympathy for labor unions had decreased, and he decided to stay and see the war out.[22]

What happened in Idaho in 1891 - 1892, though it may not have been typical, is a vivid illustration of the opposing forces in the mining wars of the West. The same people were involved in other strikes in which Pinkerton agents worked as strike breakers; this explains why Siringo was involved only in this one strike. In fact, at Gem, Idaho, during the Coeur d'Alene strike, he was recognized by a miner who had been involved in a dynamiting which Siringo had investigated earlier.

Except for the perfectly natural tendency to defend and perhaps exaggerate his own actions, Siringo seems to me to be a more than adequate reporter of what happened. The taint of his being a Pinkerton detective in the employ of the Mine Owners' Association is lessened somewhat by his sympathy for the working miner. He believed that the labor leaders were anarchists. He defended his actions, many of which seem indefensible to one sympathetic with the labor union movement, by insisting that his purpose was to oppose anarchy. And his actions, he contended, were not as bad as actions of other Pinkerton detectives. And they proved his shrewdness and cleverness. And the end justified the means. "Let us do evil that good may come." And Siringo was studying the ways of the world in order to write another book. However we might criticize his actions or admire them, his actions in the Coeur d'Alene troubles were remarkable, and his descriptions of the events seem accurate and are interesting.[23]

Siringo, after meeting with representatives of the Mine Owners' Association, went to Gem, the toughest mining camp in the district, and took a job at the Gem Mine. Only the mine superintendent knew who he really was. He appeared to be only a tough working man named C. Leon Allison, a little more educated than most and considerably tougher than the average miner. There were three mines in the town—the Gem, the Helen-Frisco, and the Black Bear. About five hundred miners worked in the three mines; the population of the town, a camp of two or three stores and half a dozen saloons, was about 1,000. Siringo patronized the saloons and gambling halls freely and was a "good fellow among the boys."

About two weeks after his arrival at Gem, Siringo joined the Gem Miners' Union. About two months later he was elected recording secretary of the union, of which George A. Pettibone was the financial secretary. Pettibone was later one of the Western Federation of Miners officials tried for the murder of Governor Steunenberg of Idaho. Siringo says Pettibone was a rabid anarchist. By the time he had become an officer in the union, Siringo had concluded that the unions were being run by "dangerous anarchists, who had completely duped the hard-working miners and were formulating demands to which the owners could not possibly agree." Others he characterized as "escaped outlaws and toughs from other States."

Siringo comments that his position in the union was a useful position; this is one of his typical understatements. He was able to make full reports on union activities to the St. Paul, Minnesota, office of Pinkerton's; the reports then would be sent back to the mine owners. Because the Gem postmaster and his assistant were both strong union sympathizers, Siringo walked to Wallace, four miles from Gem, to mail his reports, going after dark so as not to be seen (he thought).

After he became recording secretary of the union, Siringo decided to quit his job as a miner. So he began loafing on the job, was fired by the shift-boss, and thus could not get any more work in the camp. Doubtless Siringo did not enjoy the hard work in the mines. He let it be known that his rich father in Texas was supporting him and continued his work with the union; everyone was expecting trouble soon.

V *Silver Strike*

"In due course," Siringo writes, "things came to a head; the miners struck, and feeling at once became very bitter." The first action taken by the union, with Siringo participating, was to drive the nonstriking workers—"scabs"—out of town and, if possible, out of the state. People were driven out during the middle of winter, with little clothing and supplies. Siringo says he learned new lessons in human nature; other camps besides Gem were driving nonstrikers into Montana. Those in the unions who protested the inhuman treatment of the scabs felt the ire of the union leaders and soon learned to keep quiet.

In the spring of 1892, Siringo says, war was declared between the Mine Owners' Association and the Executive Committee of the Coeur d'Alene Central Organization of the Miners' Union. Pettibone, who represented the Gem Union, told Siringo that the committee had chosen a secret group of thugs to intimidate the scabs. Even if they committed murder, the union would stick by them. Nobody except the executive committee knew the identity of these men, who were paid from a union fund reserved for the good of the order.

Soon all the mines in the Coeur d'Alene were closed down. A meeting of union officials and mine owners' representatives was held at Wallace. An attempt was made to keep the mine owners' lawyer, William T. Stoll, from speaking, but finally, Siringo says, "cooler heads got control," and Stoll "was allowed to speak his little piece."

In order to keep the mines in operation, the mine owners imported a trainload of scabs. Having been warned by Siringo that the miners were waiting for the train at Wallace, those in charge, including, he says, John Hays Hammond, steamed through Wallace and unloaded the men at Burke. Hammond says other trainloads of nonunion workers followed.[24]

The violent harassing of the nonunion workers increased. Siringo says several volumes would be required to record all the cruel acts. Early in the spring he bought a rooming house and hired Mrs. Shipley, whose husband was working somewhere else, to run it for him. He built a tall board fence behind the house for protection from intruders. This house was later valuable as a hideout.

Siringo was regularly reporting union information from the meeting and union secrets supplied him by Pettibone, who had taken a fancy to him, to the mine owners. This included information that a bloody revolution was planned for July, possibly for July 4. In the meantime a mine owners' newspaper, the *Coeur d'Alene Barbarian*, published at Wardner, began publishing union secrets, including information available only to a member of the Gem Union. Siringo fell under suspicion.

So, Siringo says, a "one-eyed, two-legged, Irish hyena" from the Butte City, Montana, union, a man named Dallas (alias Tim O'Leary), came to Gem to investigate the information leaks. Within a week Dallas decided that Siringo was guilty. Johnny Murphy, a union man who liked Siringo, warned him that he was suspected; Siringo had been seen mailing too many letters at Wallace. Murphy advised Siringo to leave, but Siringo decided to stick to his guns as a true soldier would.

At a specially called meeting, either that night or the next day, after Siringo had read the minutes of the last meeting, Dallas, or O'Leary, made a speech insisting that there was a traitor in their midst and that he should not leave the meeting alive. Dallas said that the traitor could only be the man that kept the record book. There was a burst of savage applause, and Siringo, with "old Colt's .45" in a shoulder holster and a bowie knife in his belt, began planning to kill as many of the leaders as he could before he was killed.

A ten-minute recess was called while Siringo's record book was examined. A missing page was found. Siringo reminded the president, Oliver Hughes, that the page, which contained plans to flood the mines, had been removed from the book at Hughes's order (he did not tell his questioners that the page had been sent to Pinkerton's). Hughes eventually remembered the incident, and Siringo was temporarily out of danger. He believed that Dallas and others thought he would expose his guilt during Dallas's speech or (during the recess) would try to escape, but, Siringo says, he had played too much cow-camp poker.

But Siringo knew he was in danger. A day or two after the meeting Mrs. Shipley pointed out a man to him, saying that the man had been following Siringo. The man was "Black Jack" Griffin, a man who had been involved in one of Siringo's previous cases. Siringo was almost sure that he had been recognized.

Law and order no longer existed. Scabs were caught and nearly beaten to death. Mine owners who came to town barely escaped being mobbed. The mines were barricaded and guarded. Siringo was warned by a member of the union that he would be killed at the meeting of the union to be held on July 9. So Siringo did not attend the meeting; instead he turned in his resignation and the record book at the meeting hall door, giving as his reason the fact that he was not trusted by the union. At the same time he denied being a Pinkerton operative.

Siringo spent that evening making the rounds of the saloons, picking up information and trying to warn nonunion miners that they were in danger. After midnight he sneaked out through a hole in the back fence, crossed the river, and went to the Gem Mine, where he warned the manager that two of his men were to be beaten up. But he was too late. The two men had been severely beaten, and one of them was nearly dead. Siringo and one of the guards walked four miles to Wallace for the doctor. While the other guard and the doctor returned to Gem, Siringo reported to John A. Finch, secretary of the Mine Owners' Association.

Finch advised Siringo not to return to Gem, but Siringo said he had enlisted for the war and would stay and finish. The next morning, carrying his Winchester, he rode the train into Gem, along with George Pettibone and a delegation of union leaders. He backed the angry Pettibone down and marched through the angry crowd of union men to his boarding house. Siringo thought the union had planned to leave him alone until the general uprising, which was supposed to start just before daybreak the next day.

Siringo again sneaked out of town, which was heavily guarded, and reported to the Gem Mine. Early the next morning he openly went past three union guards at the bridge and reentered the town. Mrs. Shipley was horrified, telling Siringo that the trouble was to start any time. The first shot was fired at 6:00 A.M.

Siringo immediately decided to return to the Gem Mine, but found that about fifty men with Winchesters were watching for him. A general battle was in progress, with much "reckless, extravagant burning of powder" on both sides. Siringo, he writes, concluded that "war is hell, sure enough." He was caught in the middle.

Siringo then pulled back the carpet in Mrs. Shipley's room and sawed a hole in the floor large enough to permit his escape. He dropped through the hole (the front part of the store was about three feet above the ground). The only escape route was under the board sidewalk on Main Street.

From his position under the building Siringo could see his
enemy, Dallas. He was tempted to kill him but refrained, he says,
fearing that the shot would give away his hiding place. About that
time there was an explosion at the Frisco Mill. Mrs. Shipley, about
twenty minutes later, warned Siringo that now the mill was blown
up, the mob was coming after him. The mob came—Siringo says
there were about 1,000 men—but Mrs. Shipley did not reveal
Siringo's hiding place.

Siringo, afraid the mob would burn the building, crawled under
the board sidewalk, which was about a foot off the ground, with the
sidewalk above lined with miners who were looking for him. Finally
he came to a saloon which was built on pilings, with an opening at
the back. The three guards at the rear of the saloon were watching
the crowd on the street.

Siringo, pretending he was trying to get a shot at the scabs at the
Gem, went past them and entered a culvert under the high railroad
grade before the guards caught on. Pulling himself through a waist-
deep stream of rushing water, he escaped to the other side, went
under a house built over the end of the culvert, and crossed a 200-
yard open space to the Gem Mine, in danger of being shot by both
sides. But he made it safely to the Gem. His route of escape can be
traced in a picture of the main street of Gem, taken in 1892; the picture faces page 170 of *Riata and Spurs*.

Much has been written about Siringo's bravery, or lack of fear. In
writing of his escape from Gem to the mine, Siringo says,

In hurrying through this brush under the saloon my watch-chain caught
and tore loose. On it was a charm, a $3 gold piece with my initials C. L. A. I
hated to lose this, so stopped to consider as to whether I should go back and
hunt it. While studying, I wondered if I was scared. I had to smile at the
thought, so I concluded to test the matter by spitting; but bless you, my
mouth was so dry I couldn't spit anything but cotton, or what looked like
cotton. I decided that it was a case of scared with a big S. I had always
heard that when a person is badly frightened he can't spit; but this was the
first time I saw it tested.[25]

Soon the strikers warned the Gem Mine superintendent that if he
did not surrender the mill would be blown up as the Frisco mill had
been. The superintendent refused, and Siringo and some men went
up the hill and tied some heavy poles across the tramway so that a
dynamite-loaded car could not be sent down to the mill. During this

work Siringo recognized and reported two guards who were spies for the union.

Soon after that the superintendent received orders from the owners to surrender to the union. Siringo advised against the surrender, because he thought, as subsequent events proved, that the lives of the nonunion miners would be endangered. But the superintendent had to follow orders, and Siringo and one of the guards escaped to the mountains above the Coeur d'Alene Valley. For several days they hid in the mountains overlooking Gem and Wallace and observed the activities; they made one trip into Wallace, where Siringo was told that the miners were frantically searching for him. On July 14 they were in the mountains above Wallace and saw more than a thousand federal and state troops commanded by Colonel William P. Carlin take over and begin rounding up the union officials. The governor had declared martial law because of the violence.

VI *Martial Law*

Siringo and his companion immediately joined the soldiers, and Siringo spent the next few days helping round up the agitators and union leaders. Using his cowboy terminology, probably inspired by the term "bull pen," he writes that for the next week or so he was busy "putting unruly cattle in the bull pen." Soon there were more than three hundred "bulls" in the corral. Among those captured was George A. Pettibone, who had set the fuse for the blowing up of the Frisco mill and was injured in the blast, which killed several men.

Siringo eventually appeared before the grand jury which indicted the rioters and testified in the trials at Coeur d'Alene and at Boise. Eighteen union leaders, including Pettibone, were convicted, though Siringo does not tell us that the United States Supreme Court eventually reversed the convictions, freeing Pettibone and others from the penitentiary.[26]

Siringo spent fourteen months on the Coeur d'Alene operation. He writes that though he had ample opportunity to kill men and get away with doing so, he did not. Siringo's property in Gem burned early in January 1893, to the pleasure of the "union mob" and at the loss of $3,000 to Siringo. All he had to show for the operation was his weekly salary, his experience, and a better understanding of the ways of the world.

VII   *Idaho Postcript*

Siringo, so far as I can tell, was never again involved in
strikebreaking, probably because he became so well known to
miners and union leaders during the Coeur d'Alene riots and trials.
He worked on mine frauds, but mainly after 1892 he was a man
hunter. But Siringo was involved in a case involving Idaho miners
in the fall of 1906 and early in 1907. He went to Boise as James
McParland's bodyguard during the famous trial of William "Big
Bill" Haywood, secretary of the Western Federation of Miners;
Charles Moyer, president of the union; and Siringo's old friend
George Pettitbone, also a WFM official, for the murder of Governor
Steunenberg of Idaho.[27]

The background of the WFM officials' trial is bizarre. Steunenberg had declared martial law in the Coeur d'Alene strike of 1899
and was hated by many union men for his doing so. On December
30, 1905, now a private citizen, he was killed in Caldwell, Idaho, by
a bomb which exploded at the gate of his residence. Eventually
Harry Orchard was arrested and accused of the bombing. James
McParland, Denver superintendent of Pinkerton's, gained
Orchard's confidence and obtained a full confession, one which im-
plicated Haywood, Moyer, and Pettibone. The chief prosecutor was
William E. Borah, later Senator from Idaho, and the defendants'
chief lawyer was Clarence Darrow.[28]

In the fall of 1906 Siringo began traveling as McParland's
bodyguard while McParland, who was nearly blind, was trying to
assemble evidence for the trial. The rumor was that the "Western
Federation of Miners Dynamiters" had added McParland to their
list. Siringo went with McParland to the Idaho penitentiary several
times while McParland was talking to Orchard. He visited friends in
the area and looked over the scene of the crime He talked to many
people who had been involved in the Coeur d'Alene troubles. Later
he made a second trip with McParland to Idaho to witness the trial
of Steve Adams, another accused dynamiter. They spent two weeks
in Wallace, and Siringo visited scenes of the 1892 troubles.

When the trial began on May 9, 1907, Siringo was in Boise,
where he not only was Harry Orchard's guard during the trial but
was McParland's bodyguard. While the trial was in session,
McParland remained in his hotel room. In *A Cowboy Detective*
there is (facing page 511) a picture of Siringo and four other men
with Harry Orchard, whom they were guarding. There is also (fac-

ing page 514) a picture of Siringo and McParland (called McCartney), evidently taken in Boise during the trial.

The labor leaders were acquitted, probably because of the eloquence of Darrow and because of the inadequacy of the uncorroborated testimony of one man, Orchard, to convict the three men of murder. Siringo, always suspicious, believed that one of the jurors, in the employ of the Western Federation of Miners, convinced the others that if a verdict of guilty were brought, the jury would "meet a dreadful fate."

Siringo claims to have helped foil a plot to lynch Pettibone, Moyer, and Haywood, along with Clarence Darrow. Governor Gooding is supposed to have dissuaded a mob from disgracing the State of Idaho forever by lynching the men.

Siringo seems to have enjoyed being a part of the famous trial. He tells with pride of his arranging for actress Ethel Barrymore and Giffort Pinchot, Chief of the United States Forest Service, to have an interview with Orchard, who later was convicted of murder and given a life sentence. Pinchot wrote a short introduction to *Riata and Spurs*.

So Siringo was involved with his personal fight against anarchy early in his career as "the cowboy detective" as well as towards the end of his career as a Pinkerton operative (he left the agency in 1908). Although his experience among the hardrock miners, working mainly for their mine-owner employers, was a colorful part of Siringo's career, it occupied less than four years of the twenty-two years he worked for the agency. More frequently he worked alone, under an alias, chasing known outlaws and trying to solve the crimes of violence that were typical during the final period of Western settlement.

CHAPTER 9

Law and Outlaw

I *The Cowboy Detective*

SIRINGO'S first detective work was done for the LX Ranch, when he went to New Mexico in search of rustled cattle and rustlers and was involved (only incidentally) in the capture of Billy the Kid. The Lincoln County, New Mexico, War, which made both Billy the Kid and Pat Garrett famous, was both typical and symptomatic of the disorder, called by some lawlessness, which accompanied the Westward movement. The people were scattered, the traditional legal institutions were often corrupt and weak, and extralegal means of settling things were often used. The speed with which the Great Plains and Rocky Mountain area was settled, however sparsely, was also a contributing cause of lawlessness. Between 1865 and 1885, an area roughly one-fifth of the continental United States, populated mainly by buffalo and Indians, was settled, though not very thickly, by cattlemen and miners. The mountain man had virtually disappeared; Indians were rapidly being driven to the reservations, and in the Southwest especially the Mexican-American population, mainly that in the lower economic brackets, was being relegated to subserviency.

Besides the cattle rustling, present wherever the Range Cattle Industry thrived, and the political struggles through the West, other lawless acts accompanied the Westward movement after 1865. These included stagecoach and train robberies, kidnappings, and murders. Range wars, such as the Johnson County, Wyoming, War, developed between the large ranchers and the small ranchers or farmers and, less frequently, between cowman and sheepman.

Not unique but made more famous by dime novelists and writers of pulp Westerns were the outlaw gangs that roamed the West. The James and Dalton gangs were extensions of the guerrilla companies which raided the border states during the Civil War. Sam Bass and his crew seemed less regimented, more like amateurs, but they became famous through news accounts and a popular cowboy ballad. In the 1890s the famous outlaw gang was the Wild Bunch, operating out of several of the many outlaw hangouts famous in the West: the Hole in the Wall in Wyoming, Brown's Hole on the Utah-Colorado-Wyoming border, and Robber's Roost, in Utah.

Siringo spent much more time in chasing outlaws than he did in strikebreaking. As a Pinkerton cowboy detective, he could be expected to be a part of the pursuit of the Wild Bunch, and he was. Had the Pinkerton pursuit been thoroughly successful, Siringo would have added to the fame (or notoriety) which accompanied his Pinkerton activities in Idaho. But the Wild Bunch, the last of the big Western outlaw gangs, was not thoroughly vanquished. Some of the outlaws have even become folk heroes of a sort in the Hollywood search for heroes: a good example is *Butch Cassidy and the Sundance Kid*, a recent movie.

Siringo's approach (the Pinkerton approach?) to the manhunt can best be illustrated by a summary of the pursuit of a small-time criminal; most of Siringo's operations were of this sort.

II *"I'm Leavin' Cheyenne"*

In the fall of 1887 Siringo was assigned to a case in Wyoming. After conferring with District Attorney William Stoll at Cheyenne, Siringo set out in pursuit of a man named Bill McCoy, who had been convicted of killing Deputy Sheriff Gunn of Lusk, Wyoming, but had avoided hanging by a jailbreak. Stoll believed McCoy was somewhere on the Keeline cattle range on the Platt River, above old Fort Laramie. McCoy had worked there on a ranch operated by Tom Hall (really Tom Nichols), who was supposedly a fugitive from Texas, and a gang of men many of whom had escaped from the penitentiary in Texas.[1]

Siringo had been told that other detectives had been found out and had been driven out of the country; so he approached the Keeline ranch with extreme caution, while avoiding a cautious appearance. He boarded the train which ran north of Cheyenne and rode it to its northern terminus. There he bought a horse and saddle and headed ostensibly for Fort Douglas, which was about a hundred miles north. On the second day he stopped for the noon meal at "Howard's No. 5 Roundup Road Ranch," a saloon about five miles from the Keeline ranch. It was operated by an ex-policeman and saloon keeper from Cheyenne and his wife, an ex-prizefighter and dance hall girl, also from Cheyenne. It was winter; business was bad; and the Howards got drunk with Siringo, who had convinced them that he was a Texas outlaw.

About four o'clock Siringo started to leave, but a farewell drink with the Howards led to several more. Siringo, after thirty minutes, made another start, saying he hoped to meet some other Texas boys at Douglas. When Howard mentioned some Texas cowboys nearby, Siringo asked where they were. After warning him that he would probably be killed, Howard directed him to the ranch. After buying more whiskey, Siringo rode recklessly into the cottonwood timber which separated the saloon from the ranch. Then he laid out a trail for the outlaws to examine, including galloping his horse over dangerous parts of the trail and simulating a fall in the sand of an arroyo.

He rode into the camp drunk, with his "injured" leg bandaged. Some of the outlaws sympathized, but others were suspicious. They back-trailed him, read the sign as Siringo intended them to, and checked his story with the Howards. He was permitted to stay with the outlaws and was tolerated by most of them, although he did not completely gain the trust of all.

A man named McChesney, whom Siringo recognized as a Texas acquaintance of twenty years before but who thought Siringo was one of the Pumphry boys, Texas murderers, kept Siringo informed of the gang's opinions.

Finally Hall, the leader, asked Siringo if he had known Bill Gatlin in Texas. Siringo had worked with Gatlin in the Panhandle, until Gatlin got into trouble and had to skip out and change his name again. Gatlin was not his real name. Later Hall told Siringo that Bill McCoy, the fugitive, was really Bill Gatlin, and that Hall and others had engineered McCoy's jailbreak. The fugitive had left Hall's ranch two days before Siringo's arrival, on his way to New Orleans and, eventually, to Argentina.

A week later, the outlaw crew rode to a dance near Fort Laramie. While the others were drunk, Siringo rode to Laramie, rented a hotel room, wrote and mailed his first report to Pinkerton's, and returned to the dance before the crew was ready to return. On the way back to the ranch Siringo's hands were full keeping McChesney and another outlaw from killing one another.

A few days later Howard came to the ranch and reported that his wife was dying. The entire crew, including Hall and the cook, rode over to the saloon; Howard provided free liquor, and Siringo writes that "what happened would have made angels weep." Whiskey was poured down the woman's throat up to her last breath, which expired just before midnight.

Then the Irish wake began in dead earnest. It included Howard's drunken, maudlin reminiscences of when he first met the corpse and drunken cowboy songs, both nice and vulgar, sung over the corpse. The next day the corpse was put in a rough box and lowered to its last resting place, the funeral consisting of the drinking of toasts and the singing of songs. One of the songs was a parody of "The Sweet By and By," the first line of which was "There's a land that beats this one all to hell." Siringo was amused by another parody involving the Pinkerton agency:

> Oh, see the train go 'round the bend,
> Goodby, my lover, goodby.
> She's loaded down with Pinkerton men,
> Goodby, my lover, goodby.

The Howard saloon was virtually destroyed in the wake of the outlaw cyclone which struck it, the walls shot full of holes and the liquor all gone. When he sobered up, Howard left for Cheyenne, and Hall's men went back to the ranch. Siringo writes, "Of course, I didn't have as much fun as the rest, owing to the fact that I had to use one crutch."[2]

By this time Siringo was a trusted member of the outlaw gang. On other rides to Fort Laramie, forty miles away, Siringo says, "reports were written and much liquor destroyed." Siringo pretended to fall in love with a girl at the northern terminus of the railroad and rode there fairly often. After Siringo finally found out that McCoy had left New Orleans for Argentina, he rode to the railway station, sold his horse and saddle, and boarded the train for Cheyenne. There he appeared before the grand jury and testified against the Hall gang; soon the gang was arrested by the sheriff and a large posse. Hall blamed "Henderson" (Siringo), rightly, for the arrest.

Siringo waited at Denver to be called as a witness against the gang, but because of a disagreement between the district attorney and the judge, the cases never came to trial, and Siringo did not have to appear as a witness. Siringo was happy about the outcome because he thought Hall "a prince" with "a heart in him like an ox," and also sympathized with McChesney because he had known him and his father earlier.

This pattern was repeated frequently in Siringo's cowboy detective work. Like a good cowboy should, he did his work on horseback. In other cases he would pick the weakest member of a gang, gain his confidence, go on a trip (preferably a hunting trip) with him, get a confession, and then notify the agency to have them both arrested. Usually the fugitive would confess to the authorities and Siringo would disappear, go back to Denver, and go to work on another case. He used these procedures in his pursuit of the Wild Bunch, in which he was involved for most of a four-year period.

III   *The Wild Bunch*

The Wild Bunch was more than a gang of outlaws. It was the last gasp of the wild and woolly West, of the individualistic free enterprise of the outlaw. William French, educated ranchman for whom at various times most of the Wild Bunch worked, believed that these men were too high-strung to adapt themselves to a changing civilization. He believed that all of the Wild Bunch, had they been able to conceal their identity, would have become respectable citizens.[3] John H. Culley, an educated Englishman rancher, cited the cowboy badman as the last rugged individualist of the frontier.[4]

At any rate, the Wild Bunch as a gang was almost an anachronism—cowboy badmen who robbed trains and banks (which some saw as symbols of the decline of the Old West) after there were few old-time cowboys left. Indeed, the end of the free life of the open range may have been one of the causes of the existence of the Wild Bunch. It is fitting, then, that the last large cowboy outlaw gang should be pursued by cowboy detectives out of the Denver office, among them Charlie Siringo.

Actually, the Wild Bunch was made up of men who were originally involved in rustling in Wyoming and adjoining states in the 1890s. Four of the inner circle of the Wild Bunch (the three Logans and Flat-Nose Curry) were followers of Nathan Champion, who was killed by the ranchers' army in the Johnson County, Wyoming, War of 1892.[5] When rustling cattle became so hazardous as to make that occupation impracticable, the Bunch turned to robbing banks and trains. Working out of the Hole in the Wall, Brown's Hole, and Robber's Roost, the Wild Bunch, sometimes consisting of a large crew, was active in the 1890s and the first few years of the twentieth century. They rode long distances, often pursued by relentless posses and Pinkerton detectives, ranging from

Wyoming to Fort Worth and San Antonio, Texas, to Arkansas and
Mississippi, and even to New York City. The story of the Wild
Bunch is long and involved; many accounts are based on folklore
and speculation. A systematic, coherent, well-documented account
of the Wild Bunch's escapades is yet to be written.[6]

The "inner circle" of the Wild Bunch consisted of George Le Roy
Parker (Butch Cassidy), the leader; Harvey Logan (Kid Curry);
Johnny Logan; Lonny Logan; Flat-Nose George Curry; Harry
Longbaugh (the Sundance Kid); Bill (Will) Carver (Tom O'Day);
O. C. Hanks (Deaf Charlie); Harry Tracy; Bob Lee, cousin to the
Logans; Elza Lay; and Ben Kilpatrick (the Tall Texan). The chief
female hangers-on to the Bunch were Laura Bullion and Etta Pace.[7]

The most famous picture of the most famous five (Longbaugh,
Kilpatrick, Cassidy, Carver, and Harvey Logan) was taken on one of
their visits to Fort Worth. They were recognized coming out of the
studio by a detective, and within hours the Pinkerton National
Detective Agency and various law enforcing agencies had copies of
the portrait, which soon appeared on wanted posters throughout the
country. In the picture the men are neatly dressed in "town
clothes," and all wear derbies![8]

Siringo was detailed to the Wild Bunch case in early summer
1899, and he chased various members of the gang for four years.[9]
The Pinkerton National Detective Agency at various times had
many different men assigned to the chase. Siringo's account thus
gives us only a small part of what was going on. Horan, however,
gives Siringo credit for much of the success, however ephemeral, in
containing the Bunch's activities.[10]

In the summer of 1899 Siringo and W. O. Sayles went on the trail
of train robbers for the Union Pacific Railroad Company; one of its
trains had been robbed at Wilcox, Wyoming, by a gang thought to
be the Hole-in-the-Wall gang (the Wild Bunch). The loot was a
large amount of new, unsigned currency. In escaping the law the
robbers killed the sheriff. Siringo and Sayles outfitted themselves in
Denver. Their instructions were to buy horses and saddles in Salt
Lake City and ride to Brown's Park (Brown's Hole), Colorado, just
over the Utah line, where the robbers were supposedly headed.

After making the 500-mile trip by train to Salt Lake City, the two
men consulted with a friend who was a special agent for the Rio
Grande Western Railway. The agent had received information that
two of the robbers had passed Hanksville, Utah, going south.

The detectives telegraphed (in code) for permission to go by train

to Marysville, Utah, to intercept the robbers at the Dandy Crossing
Ferry on the Colorado. The superintendent told them to follow the
original instructions; so they headed south through Emigration
Canyon, over a range of mountains, and down Strawberry Creek to
the Duchesne River, eventually arriving at Fort Duchesne after a
five days' hard ride (with time taken off for good fishing on Strawberry Creek).

At Fort Duchesne they found that the Pinkerton superintendent
had changed his mind. They were to ride south after the two men
whom they had originally intended to cut off at the ferry. So they
headed south for Price, Utah, which they reached after a three-
days' ride. The next morning they left in a downpour and got only
five miles from Price when they were halted by high water between
two creeks. They returned to Price about nightfall. There their hotel
was surrounded by a posse; the possemen thought they were the
U.P. train robbers. Siringo and Sayles eventually convinced the
posse that they were merely prospectors. After three days of hard
riding in very wet weather, they arrived at Hanksville, Utah, where
the suspected train robbers had been seen.

At Hanksville they found out that two suspicious characters driving thirteen horses had crossed the Colorado at Dandy Crossing ten
days previously. Only three days before, another man with five
horses had crossed the river; this man answered the description of
Kid Curry (Harvey Logan). The detectives followed the trail of the
second man but lost it in a rocky canyon. So they followed the trail
of the other two men.

They arrived at Bluff City, Utah, on the San Juan River after a
120-mile ride, and found that not only were they now two weeks
behind the robbers but that they were three days behind two other
Pinkerton operatives who had joined the chase. Siringo writes,

Sayles and I figured that we were born leaders of men, hence we didn't like
the idea of bringing up the rear, three days behind the other two
operatives. Therefore, in Mancos, Colorado, on the Denver and Rio Grande
railroad we put our jaded horses in a pasture and stored our camp outfit,
taking our saddles along with us, and boarded a train for Durango. Here we
overtook Garman and his chum [the other two detectives]. From Durango,
Sayles and I led the chase by riding on trains, in buggies, and on hired saddle horses. We left the other two boys far in the rear, and they finally lost
the trail entirely and returned to Denver.[11]

After losing the trail several times and following false leads in

Southern Colorado and Northern New Mexico, the men separated, Siringo finally finding the trail again and Sayles looking for the stolen money in Montana.

Following the trail down the Arkansas River, Siringo arrived at Dodge City, where he spent a half-day noting the changes in the town. Then, on horseback, in buggies, and on trains, Siringo trailed the men to Wichita and Caldwell, Kansas, where he found time to visit with old friends. Then he followed the men from Caldwell to Arkansas City, Kansas, then to Winfield, and finally down the Arkansas to Fort Smith, Arkansas. By this time he had been joined by another detective.

From Fort Smith they followed the robbers to Hot Springs, where they lost the trail and split up. The other operative thought he had found the men at Nashville, Tennessee, and Siringo joined him (by way of St. Louis, where he visited his sister) only to find that the lead was false.

Back in Hot Springs, Siringo again took up a trail that by now was very cold. An "old moonshiner" put him "on the right trail" of the robbers, to Little Rock and then down the Arkansas to Stuttgart. After chasing the robbers up and down the Mississippi, Siringo finally lost them (or, as he put it, he was three weeks behind them) and was called back to Denver and reassigned to another phase of the same case.

Sayles had discovered that Kid Curry's brother "Loney" (Lonny) and his cousin Bob were running a saloon in Harlin, Montana, and had cashed some of the unsigned bills from the Wilcox, Wyoming, robbery. He had also discovered that their real names were Harvey and Lonny Logan. They had sold out and "skipped out" before Sayles had had a chance to have them arrested. The Logans had for some years made their headquarters in the Little Rockies, about fifty miles east of Harlin.

The plan was for Siringo to buy an outfit at Great Falls, Montana, and ride about 250 miles across the Badlands to Landusky, a small cattle town in the Little Rockies. So from Great Falls Siringo rode to Lewiston in three days. Since it was late in February, a severe snowstorm was in progress. After waiting for two days Siringo, more impatient than usual, started out; the wind was "blowing a gale," and the temperature was twenty below zero. Because of the cold weather he turned aside to a mining camp called Gilt Edge instead of traveling to Rocky Point. The next day he rode to the Red Barn ranch on the south border of the Badlands, where he waited for a chinook (a warm wind) before going to Rocky Point, where he learned more about the Curry gang. Kid Curry, he found out, was half-owner of a horse ranch in the Little Rockies, his partner being "Jim Thompson."

Siringo made friends with Thompson in Landusky and, as Charles L. Carter, "an old Mexico outlaw," he gained the confidence of the outlaw element in the community. He became friends with Elfie Landusky, daughter of the town founder's widow (Kid Curry had killed Landusky); Elfie was the common-law wife of Lonny Logan, who had recently been killed in Missouri by the Pinkertons. By reading Elfie's letters he gained much information about the Logans.

Soon after he arrived in Landusky Siringo was in a stagecoach accident in the icy waters of the Milk River. In June he was almost killed when a team of wild horses belonging to Thompson ran away with a buckboard and overturned it. He managed to make it back to Thompson's ranch (his back and head were injured), where he spent three weeks recovering from the accident and, typically, learning much about Kid Curry and the other Logans. Among other information, he learned that Kid Curry (Harvey Logan) had planned to rob another U.P. train, and that Flat-Nose George Curry (who was not kin to the other "Currys") was one of the Wilcox train robbers. The Pinkertons sent word to Siringo that Flat-Nose George was in Chihuahua, Mexico.

So Siringo, because the Pinkertons did not expect that Kid Curry would return to the Little Rockies, was called back to Denver. But they were wrong, because not long after Siringo left Thompson's ranch in August, Curry returned and killed a rancher named Winters, who had killed Curry's brother, Johnny Logan. In A Cowboy Detective, Siringo says that William Pinkerton believed that Jim Thompson was really "Dad" Jackson, Sam Bass's henchman, but Riata and Spurs gives no such speculation.

Siringo and another operative went to El Paso, where the other man waited until Siringo sought to locate Flat-Nose George Curry. By train and on horseback, Siringo picked up the trail, but within two weeks had determined that the Mexico suspect was not Flat-Nose George, who was killed soon after in Utah.

When he arrived at Denver after his trip to Mexico Siringo found that the information he got from Thompson was accurate; the Wild Bunch had struck again, this time holding up the U.P. train at Tipton, Wyoming. One of the Pinkerton officials had determined that

Kid Curry, Longbaugh, and another man had pulled the job. As a result of a tip that Kid Curry and a tall companion had been seen south of Grand Junction, Colorado, Siringo was assigned to follow them.

Siringo rode the Denver and Rio Grande train to Grand Junction, bought a saddle horse and a pack horse, and headed south. He soon found out, at a ranch south of Grand Junction, that he was only a week behind the train robbers. At Paradox Valley, where the "notorious Young boys" were from, he learned that Lafe Young, an outlaw, had left with the robbers. Siringo stayed around Paradox Valley for a week and, after starting out on one false trail, headed south through unsettled country for the Blue Mountains of Southern Utah.

There he found that the train robbers, who had failed to get any money on the last holdup, were headed south. Siringo made friends with a gang of outlaws at Indian Creek, saw Robber's Roost from afar, and visited Monticello, Utah. From the Blue Mountains he rode south to Bluff City, on the San Juan River, then west to Dandy Crossing on the Colorado (in the present area of Lake Powell), getting lost for two days. From Dandy Crossing he went north to Hanksville, where he and Sayles had visited earlier. As he was leaving Hanksville, a traveling photographer photographed Siringo and his traveling outfit. The picture is the frontispiece to *Riata and Spurs*.

From Hanksville, at the suggestion of one of the Pinkerton officials, he drifted west toward the Sevier Valley, where Butch Cassidy was "born and raised." First he spent the night at Cainsville, on the Dirty Devil River, and then started west. He found the snow too deep to travel, walked fifteen miles chasing his runaway horses, and almost got lost, finally spending the night at an isolated ranch house.

Several days traveling over the mountains brought him to Circleville, on the Sevier River, where he spent a week finding out about Butch Cassidy's early life. Cassidy's real name was George Le Roy Parker; his nickname was "Sallie." Siringo says this nickname itself was enough to drive a sensitive boy to the bad. Siringo admits that he nearly fell in love with Cassidy's sister, who was the deputy postmistress at Circleville.

From Circleville Siringo rode south to Pangwitch and then to Kanab, on the Arizona line, where he "laid in a good supply of grub." From Kanab he rode southeast, crossing the Colorado at

Lee's Ferry, where, he says, "green alfalfa was a foot high and the flowers and the combs on the chickens were in full bloom." From Lee's Ferry he went to the Indian trading store at Willow Creek and then turned due east through the Navajo and Moqui reservations, looking always for the Wild Bunch. After spending two weeks among the Indians, he crossed the Atlantic and Pacific Railroad at Gallup, New Mexico, then turned south through Zuni country to a salt lake near the Arizona line.

Then he rode south, through American Valley and Luna Valley, where he fell in with "many tough characters" and learned more about the Wild Bunch. Finally Siringo reached "the sleepy little town" of Alma, New Mexico, having traveled more than 1,000 miles on horseback. "The town of Alma," he writes, "supported one store and one saloon, both being well patronized by the wild and woolly population thinly scattered over the surrounding country."

Siringo "made himself solid with the tough element of the district," seeking to find out more about the Wild Bunch and about who had passed some of the unsigned money stolen in the Wilcox, Wyoming, train robbery. Previously a Pinkerton assistant superintendent, Frank Murray, had gone into the area to find out about the matter. Since there were no local officers to help him, Murray confided in the storekeeper and the saloonkeeper, who was named Jim Lowe. That night Murray was driven out of town; he would have been killed except for the intercession of Jim Lowe, who, Siringo later found out, was really Butch Cassidy. Lowe—or Cassidy—had sold his saloon and "hit the trail for tall timber" the day after the detective's exit.

Siringo also spent time in detective work at the Mogollon mining camp; at Graham, another mining town; and at Frisco, a cattle town near the Arizona line. At Frisco he obtained information that Jim Lowe and eight companions had established a "robber's roost" about forty miles southwest of Frisco and were getting ready for some sort of raid. He wrote to Pinkerton's, to the assistant superintendent, Murray, telling of plans to visit the outlaw camp and to try to infiltrate the gang. He received a reply from Murray saying that Jim Lowe was not Cassidy. Murray had met Lowe and had found him to be a nice gentleman. He instructed Siringo to sell his horses and return to Denver for reassignment to another area. Siringo comments wryly that Murray's putting a stop to his visiting Cassidy may have been a godsend; he might have been killed. On the other hand, possibly the gang might have been killed or captured.

Siringo followed orders without protest. He sold his horses at the Mogollon mining camp and boarded the stagecoach for Silver City, about eighty miles away. Also on the stagecoach was Blake Graham, Jim Lowe's friend, who confirmed Siringo's information that Lowe was really Cassidy. But Siringo evidently said no more to Murray about Lowe's real identity.

After visiting his daughter at Silver City and spending a day at his ranch at Santa Fe, Siringo returned to Denver and was immediately sent to Grand Junction, Colorado, to locate a man named Jim Foss, a member of the Wild Bunch. Siringo found Foss, who was farming a small patch of land near Palisade, twenty miles above Grand Junction.

Foss had received a warning that a Pinkerton detective was on his trail—in fact Siringo brought him the letter—and he swore bloody vengeance against all detectives.

Siringo, who called himself Lee Roy Davis, had come prepared. He had managed to get an account of his being in a shooting scrape in southern New Mexico printed in the newspapers, and he carried clippings showing that he was wanted in New Mexico. Foss was convinced; when he, in August, "pulled out for tall timber," Siringo was with him. Living off the land, they drifted north to Hayden, Colorado, and then to Dixon, Wyoming, the town the vigilantes had chased Foss out of. At Dixon, Siringo and Foss had decided to go to Rawlins to meet some of Foss's friends, when one of Foss's friends warned him (again) that Pinkertons were on his trail. So Foss sold Siringo his pack horse and outfit and headed back toward Grand Junction. He gave Siringo a letter of introduction to a friend in Rawlins (Siringo was now named Harry Blevins). The letter stated simply, "This will introduce to you my friend Harry Blevins. He is righter than hell."

So Siringo "pulled out" for "the hurrah little city of Rawlins, where half the men are railroad employees and the other half, with the exception of gamblers and saloon men, smell sheepy." There he learned more about the Wild Bunch from Foss's saloonkeeper friend. Siringo spent the winter in Rawlins, leading "a hurrah drinking life." He made friends with a closemouthed young man named Bert, who was virtually one of the Wild Bunch but who was bright enough to keep himself out of the clutches of the authorities. In the spring he went with Bert to Grand Junction, Colorado, 300 miles away, on horseback; there they hobnobbed with Bert's tough cowboy friends, including Foss.

While he was in Grand Junction, Siringo traveled to Santa Fe on business, and Foss asked him to give a Wild Bunch cipher code to a man named Bob McGinnis in the Santa Fe penitentiary and to tell him that the Wild Bunch would have him out of the pen before long. McGinnis was really Elza Lay of the Wild Bunch. With help from New Mexico officials in getting to see McGinnis, Siringo gave the code to the prisoner (and, of course, to the authorities). While Siringo was in Santa Fe, Butch Cassidy, Bill Carver, and Harry Longbaugh robbed the Winnemucca, Nevada, bank of $30,000 in gold. It was plain, Siringo thought, that some of the money would be used to help free McGinnis.

In early summer Siringo, Bert, and Bert's younger brother headed across country, with a pack outfit, to Rawlins. At a ranch on the Wyoming border they heard of the robbery of the Denver and Rio Grande train east of Grand Junction (Bert's friend Bill Cruzon was in the hold-up gang), and from then on, Siringo and the other two were suspected of the holdup. In Dixon, Bert was warned that a detective named Siringo was infiltrating the Wild Bunch. Bert became suspicious of Siringo, who assured him blandly that he had never heard of Charlie Siringo.

Bert had reason to be concerned; Siringo had overcome Bert's being closemouthed. Bert had revealed to Siringo (and thus to the detective agency) many of the secrets of the Wild Bunch, including their "blind post-office" system throughout the West.

Time was running out for the Wild Bunch. While Siringo was in Rawlins, the Tall Texan (Kilpatrick) and Kid Curry's sweetheart, Laura Bullion, were arrested in Nashville for passing some stolen bills. Curry made his escape and came to Rawlins to dig up some of the stolen Great Northern money to hire lawyers for Laura's defense. He was in Rawlins only two days; Siringo found out about his being there two days after he went back east. Siringo says that Curry spotted him, however, and expressed a suspicion that he was a detective.

Curry was arrested in Knoxville, Tennessee, and convicted for passing stolen money. He escaped from the Knoxville jail, however. A man believed to be Kid Curry was killed by officers after the robbery of a Denver and Rio Grande train at Parachute, Colorado, on June 7, 1904, although Siringo did not believe he was really Kid Curry.[12] Kilpatrick and Laura Bullion received long federal prison terms. Most of the ringleaders of the Wild Bunch were either captured or killed in the United States. The main exceptions were Butch Cassidy and the Sundance Kid (Harry Longbaugh), who sailed from New York to Argentina early in 1901, where they were later killed, according to Pinkerton operatives, in Bolivia, in 1912.[13]

There has been considerable controversy over whether or not Cassidy and the Sundance Kid were really killed in Bolivia. Like Jesse James and Billy the Kid, Cassidy was hard to kill. Evidence of Jesse James's death at the hand of Robert Ford seems certain, but Billy the Kid and Butch Cassidy are harder to put to rest. Horan, in the preface to *The Wild Bunch*, acknowledged the rumors of Cassidy's still being alive and wrote, "Well, Butch, if you're reading this . . . you might drop me a line."

Charles Kelly, in the revised edition of *The Outlaw Trail; a History of Butch Cassidy and His Wild Bunch*, included a chapter entitled "Is Butch Cassidy Dead?" He examined all of the accounts of Cassidy's current vitality and concluded that Cassidy died as reported. He accepted the statement of Mrs. William T. Phillips (Phillips has often been cited as being Cassidy), who said that Phillips was not really Cassidy but merely Butch's good friend. Kelly also wrote that statements in Phillips's death certificate "proved positively that Phillips was not Cassidy."

Lula Parker Betenson's *Butch Cassidy, My Brother* (as told to Dora Flack), after the movie on Cassidy and the Sundance Kid was made, wrote a book about Cassidy, in general giving the usually accepted details of Cassidy's life. She said that Cassidy had returned to his old stomping grounds and had visited with friends and relatives. She insisted, however, that William T. Phillips was not Butch Cassidy. She had promised never to reveal his assumed name. It is significant, however, that when she wrote her book she was the only survivor among the family who allegedly had seen Cassidy alive when he was supposed to have returned home. The testimony of one person, not a disinterested one, is hardly definitive.

In 1977 Larry Pointer published *In Search of Butch Cassidy*, a masterful attempt to prove that Cassidy, as William T. Phillips, lived beyond his reported death date. The proof Pointer submitted is the absence of mention of Phillips or his ancestors in public records before May 1908, when he was married, using the name of William T. Phillips; a ring given by Phillips to one of Cassidy's former girl friends, containing the inscription "Geo C to Mary B"; a revolver owned by Phillips which had Cassidy's brand on it; the

testimony of several old-timers who knew both men; the testimony
of Lula Parker Betenson, who said Cassidy lived a long life but was
not Phillips; an analysis of the handwriting of the two men from
specimens written thirty years apart; a comparison of the
photographs of Cassidy (taken in 1894) and Phillips (taken about
1930).

This "evidence" is not foolproof. The ring and revolver evidence
could have been contrived. The old-timers were not disinterested
witnesses. If Mrs. Betenson, when she said that Phillips was *not*
Cassidy, lied, how could her testimony be valid otherwise?
Handwriting analysis is not an exact science. And the two pictures,
despite "expert" analysis, seem to me to be merely pictures of men
who looked alike. Absence of a scar on Phillips's forehead and dif-
ferences of ear structure are explained by hypothetical plastic
surgery!

Pointer pointed out that there could no longer be any question
that Phillips was Cassidy. I remain unconvinced; more proof is
needed, despite Pointer's conclusions. Phillips's manuscript on the
life of Butch Cassidy did not make the claim that Phillips was
Cassidy; there is good reason to believe that he was not.

Whether or not Cassidy died in South America, Siringo had about
finished his part in the chase. After locating two men involved with
the Wild Bunch, one in Rodeo, Arizona, and the other in Gunnison,
Colorado, he returned to Denver. He had worked on the case for
four years and had traveled "more than 25,000 miles by rail, vehi-
cles, afoot, and on horseback." His main achievements were his
gaining information about the Wild Bunch for the extensive Pinkerton files. His skill in adapting himself to outlaw life was his chief
asset. Although Kid Curry had to be convinced that Siringo was not
a detective, Sheriff McDaniels of Rawlins believed him to be a wanted man and even went to Denver to check Pinkerton's rogue's
gallery. He did not, Siringo writes, find anyone to fit his complex-
ion.

Siringo believed that Pinkerton's made two mistakes in their han-
dling Siringo's part in the case. The first one was in not letting
Sayles and Siringo intercept the outlaws at Dandy Crossing, and the
other was in not pursuing Jim Lowe and his gang when Siringo first
identified Lowe as Butch Cassidy. But Siringo realistically agreed
that different decisions in both cases could have been very
dangerous for him.

IV *Other Detective Work*

Siringo's crusades against anarchy and his pursuit of the Wild Bunch, of course, did not occupy all of the twenty-two years he spent with Pinkerton's, but they do reveal his methods, including his fearless infiltration of the ranks of the pursued. The label his enemies gave him—"Pinkerton spy"—seems peculiarly fitting.

In order to get a full picture of Siringo's twenty-two years with the Pinkerton National Detective Agency, one must read *A Cowboy Detective*, which is the most detailed account of those years. The original *Riata and Spurs* sometimes gives additional information and is especially useful in determining the real names of persons and places.

The regular detective activities of Siringo included man hunts, investigations of bank robberies and train holdups, checking up on railroad employees, mine saltings, dynamitings, ore robberies at the mines, hunting for missing persons, chasing cattle rustlers, murder investigations, kidnapping investigations, and investigation of arson. These cases carried Siringo as far away from Denver as Alaska and the Cumberland Mountain area of Eastern Kentucky and Southwest Virginia.

One of the more interesting cases on which Siringo worked was the investigation of the kidnapping and murder of Edward Wentz, son of a Philadelphia millionaire. This investigation, in 1903, took Siringo to Letcher County, Kentucky, and Wise County, Virginia, in what Siringo accurately calls moonshiner country. Siringo's geography and description of the people are accurate. (I spent several years in the area.) The area which Siringo traveled was the setting of novels about the mountain feuds written by John Fox, Jr., during the first decade of the twentieth century. Siringo even reports a ballad stanza—evidently a "floating stanza"—which much later appeared in a hillbilly song written (supposedly) and recorded by Vernon Dalhart in 1924; this very popular song of the 1920s was "The Prisoner's Song."[14]

Most of Siringo's activities for Pinkerton's, although he later insisted that the methods of the detective agency promoted anarchy, were on the side of law and involved the pursuit of outlaws. It can be seen, however, that Siringo's ethics were at best situation ethics. He believed that the end justifies the means. His success greatly depended on his almost uncanny ability to lie with a straight face.

His frequent falling in and out of love in the line of duty, to gain information for the Pinkerton files, while not a dominant motif of *A Cowboy Detective*, is very noticeable.

A special time—the end of the open range—and a special economic situation—the dearth of employment for the old-time cowboy, who became an anachronism in the late 1880s—were probably the factors which caused Siringo to remain with Pinkerton's as long as he did. And, he always insisted, he was learning about life. Also, he took pride in the fact that he was the *cowboy* detective.

CHAPTER 10

The End of the Trail

I Santa Fe

IN 1891, while on an investigation in New Mexico, Siringo was attracted to the state and its inhabitants and was especially pleased with the climate of Santa Fe. So he bought a tract of land near the edge of town, established a residence, and called it the Sunny Slope Ranch.[1] His wife, Mamie, had died the preceding winter,[2] and evidently Siringo was looking for some symbol of stability. During the next few years, while he was working for Pinkerton's, he returned to the ranch whenever he could.

After the Haywood trial at Boise, when Siringo and McParland returned to Denver, Siringo resigned from the Pinkerton National Detective Agency, saying that his twenty-two years' schooling had taught him all he wanted to know (he could have said more than he wanted to know) about the ways of the world. McParland offered him a position as superintendent of one of the western branches, but he refused the offer, as he had previously turned down similar offers. There was, Siringo said, "not enough kick in office work."

So, in late August 1907 Siringo returned to Santa Fe, to his Sunny Slope ranch, which was being operated by Siringo's foreman, George Tweedy. Here Siringo, the gentleman rancher, California style, took delight in helping milk the fine-blooded Jersey cows and care for the White Leghorn chickens and homer pigeons. Siringo writes, "When the work was done, I could have the Mexican servant, Ben Romero, put my saddle on either Rowdy or Patsy, offspring of Lulu Edson, and start for a gallop over the cactus-covered plains to enjoy seeing Eat-'em-up Jake and his mate, a Russian wolfhound female, pick up jack rabbits and coyotes."[3]

Siringo's taste of real heaven lasted only a month. He went to South Dakota and worked a few months on a rustling case for the state livestock association. Then he worked on an ore-stealing case

131

for a Nevada mining firm for eight months. In 1910 he investigated
a bank robbery in Morencia, Arizona, which he believed had been
pulled off by Kid Curry. In 1912 and 1913 he made a trip to his old
haunts in Texas, his main purpose being to establish the history and
the route of the Chisholm Trail. During these years Siringo was
writing *A Cowboy Detective* and fighting with Pinkerton's over its
publication and, eventually, writing and printing *Two Evil Isms.*

In early spring, 1916, Siringo became a Ranger, with a commis-
sion as Mounted Police for the Cattle Sanitary Board of New Mexico. His headquarters was at Carrizozo, in Lincoln County; his job,
which lasted two years, involved chasing cattle rustlers and horse
thieves.[4]

In December 1922, ill with pleurisy, Siringo sold everything he
had at Santa Fe and moved to San Diego, California, to live with his
daughter, Viola Reid, and his granddaughter, Margaret. His
daughter took care of him for three months, until he was able to
move to Los Angeles, then to Hollywood. There he lived in a cabin
built especially for him behind the house of a close friend. Over his
door was a sign, "Siringo's Den."[5]

Siringo spent his last years writing *Riata and Spurs* and "The Bad
Men Cowboys." He was interviewed for a newspaper article and for
magazine articles by Neil M. Clark and Eugene Manlove Rhodes
and was visited by William S. Hart and other Hollywood notables.
He died in Hollywood on October 8, 1928.[6]

II *Evaluation*

Siringo's importance in the literature of the Southwest, especially
in literature of the Range Cattle Industry, seems established. Neil
M. Clark wrote in 1929,

Down in the State University at Austin, Texas, they have dedicated six
bronze tablets to men representing the forces which went into the building
of that state; on one of the six is inscribed simply: "Charlie Cowboy."

Those who know the literature of the cowboy's West need no introduction to "Charlie Cowboy," or, to give him his full name, Charles A. Siringo.
The very name is synonymous with every vivid phase of the old West that
is now history: buffalo-hunting, cow-punching, Indian fighting, the
Chisholm Trail, broncho-busting, Billy the Kid, No-Man's Land, John
Wesley Hardin, sheep and cattle wars, rustling, sharpshooting, prairie fires,
stampedes. Few lived as fully and daringly as Charles Siringo the varied life
of those colorful days; few went so far afield and knew so many of the men,
both good and bad, whose names are indelibly symbols of their generation
and place, and none, probably, has told so well, out of a wealth of first-

hand experience, the thrilling and romantic story as it really happened.[7]

J. Frank Dobie wrote that "no other cowboy ever talked about himself so much in print; few had more to talk about."[8] Siringo's *A Texas Cow Boy* was the first of almost 100 full-length autobiographies by men who had worked as cowboys between 1865 and 1885, the heyday of the Range Cattle Industry. Although the value of the cowboy reminiscence has been questioned,[9] these autobiographies have told us more about the Cattle Kingdom as it was than have all the formal histories. And they are infinitely more interesting and readable.

That Siringo should have become a writer is at first glance remarkable. His education was limited, and his perception should have been limited also—but it was not. He was able to see in 1883, when he quit working for wages as a cowboy, that an era was ending, that he had been a part of a frontier movement that had radically changed the life of a great portion of the country, that people were interested in cowboy life, and that he could write interestingly about his own life as a cowboy.

The success of *A Texas Cow Boy* convinced Siringo, who was easily convinced, that he could write other successful books. The opposition of the powerful Pinkerton National Detective Agency did not dissuade him. He believed that what he had done and was doing was interesting and significant, and he was right. His books, though Siringo probably did not write them with high social purpose, do add much to the history of the development of the American West from 1865 to 1920.

III   *Critical Opinion*

Since *Riata and Spurs* was Siringo's first book published by a national publisher, it was the first one to be reviewed extensively. Although a few reviewers criticized his restraint, none of the reviews which I read questioned his reliability. The qualities emphasized by most of the writers were his restraint, the scope of his information, his accuracy and authenticity, his superiority to or at least his difference from pulp writers, his humor, and his use of the language of the range.

Jim Tully, in the *New York World*, thought the book had many excellent qualities, since it was written by a man who still retained the mind and the outlook of the cowboy. However, he thought that if Siringo had been born a great writer he would have written a good book of the West.[10] B. W. Smith, Jr., in the *New York Evening*

Post Literary Review, thought he should have elaborated more. It was a mistake, he thought, to try to tell it all in one book, since the crowded action of Siringo's seventy-two years could be but roughly outlined in 276 pages. Whole epics were left hanging in the air, with but a slight mention of them in passing. Plots for a dozen dime novels were neglected. Siringo did not even describe himself. Yet, Smith conceded, in telling his story his own way, Siringo managed to leave an unforgettable picture of himself.[11]

William Rose Benet emphasized Siringo's restraint; he believed *Riata and Spurs* was a human, personal history, of great value to the historian. He emphasized the book's frankness and simplicity. The tale, he believed, was graphic and real; it could be the basis of dozens of Westerns.[12]

Owen P. White compared Siringo's book with "Western stuff" and tried to describe his humor. The book, he thought, since it was written by a man who knew the West as it was, should come as a relief from ordinary "Western stuff." It was, he believed, more authentic than most and was filled with good humor.[13]

A reviewer in the *American Review of Reviews* wrote of the scope of the book. He thought that it would be hard to find a novel or movie film containing more daredevil episodes or hairbreadth escapes than does *Riata and Spurs.* It was both autobiography and good history.[14] J. Frank Dobie wrote of its accuracy and scope, as well as its humor:

The new book, "Riata and Spurs," is a remarkably faithful and graphic history of perhaps the most representative cowboy now living—just a "fool cowboy" who never became a cowman, a "waddie" without cares or responsibilities, reckless, as tough as rawhide, as honest as daylight, as ingenious as an old saddle horse, as wise as the rattle-bearing serpent of the plains. . . . "Charlie" Siringo took part in about every phase of range experience there was to take part in. . . . "Riata and Spurs" is not only a history of facts; it is a revelation of character, an interpretation of the psychology of the always interesting old-time cowboy. It is saturated with humor. Above all, it is written without the least strain for effect or the least playing up of the most adventuresome and hazardous work that any American frontier has known.[15]

Walter Prescott Webb criticized Siringo's style and the scope of the book and analyzed his humor; the style, he thought, was direct, and the book was filled with the half-unconscious Western humor that defies imitation.[16]

As Webb has said, Siringo's good humor, including his use of the wild, preposterous metaphor and of understatement, has made his writing interesting and readable. Most of the time his style is simple and direct; his was the life of the cowboy and he spoke the language of the cowboy. His style is Western colloquial, direct, matter-of-fact, and full of humor, containing more understatement than exaggeration. He claimed to have no literary style: he said he merely told what he knew. In the closing lines of *A Texas Cow Boy* he writes,

Now, dear reader in bidding you adieu, will say: should you not be pleased with the substance of this book, I've got nothing to say in defense, as I gave you the best I had in my little shop, but before you criticise it from a literary standpoint, bear in mind that the writer had fits until he was ten years of age and hasn't fully recovered from the effects.[17]

Although Siringo disregarded "correct" usage and "literary" style, he wrote clearly. He wrote as he spoke, and since it was not necessary to be verbose in order to make people understand him when he spoke, he thought it unnecessary to be wordy when he wrote. His sentences are usually short and concise, with none of the wordiness which characterized some of the later cowboy biographers and "cowboy story" writers. An example of his restraint is the following account of a "close call" he had:

That spring I was put out of active business. I was seated on the ground by the camp-fire smoking, late in the evening, when Sam Grant, a "nigger" killer, rode up and dismounted. Picking up my pistol, which lay on the opposite side of the fire from where I was sitting, he examined it, then threw it away, at the same time pulling his pistol, with the remark, "Why don't you have a good one like mine!" He then fired at my heart.

My hands were clamped around my left leg—the knee being on a level with my heart. The large dragoon bullet struck the knee going through and lodging near the skin on the opposite side. He was raising the pistol as though to fire again when a negro cowboy, Lige, galloped into the camp out of the heavy timber and brush. This, no doubt, saved my life. Grant swore to Lige, who had dismounted and was holding me up with one hand, that his pistol went off accidentally. Then Grant galloped away saying he would send a doctor from Deming's Bridge Post-Office, the old Rancho Grande headquarters.

The doctor came late at night and cut the bullet out. Lige assisted me to the Yeamans ranch a few miles below the creek.[18]

How would the pulp Western writer have described such a
scene—or would he have described it at all? Siringo breaks several
traditions. First, the hero is careless; he is seated by the fire, with
his pistol off and out of reach. Second, the villain does not conform
to type; instead of being rough and tough, he is merely cowardly,
since the appearance of a Negro cowboy keeps him from killing the
hero. Third, the man who saves the hero is a Negro cowboy; Negro
cowboys (and there were many) are seldom mentioned in Western
literature. Fourth, the hero, instead of swearing vengeance, is glad
to get out of the scrape alive. The difference between Siringo and
the pulp writer is that Siringo relates interesting facts while the
"Western" writer writes an interesting "story."

Another incident which the shoot-'em-up Western writer would
have made much of is a fight Siringo had in Chicago. He tells it
simply; the style is vernacular and slangy, but direct:

The mix-up took place at Barnum's circus near the ticket wagon, when the
great crowd was scrambling to buy tickets to the circus. A large man, who
would have made two of me, tried to be fresh and I called him down. He
made a pass to put me to sleep the first punch but before he could get in his
work the weight of my old Colt's 45 pistol had landed on his head. This was
followed up with one more lick which buried the sharp pistol-sight into his
skull. This brought the blood in a stream. By this time his partner had
picked up a piece of board and had raised it to strike me from the rear. I
saw him just in time. He found a cocked pistol in his face, and dropping the
board, begged for mercy.[19]

An example of Siringo's use of understatement is found in his account of another fight which occurred in Denver. In it he uses the
passive voice, which serves to make bloody action almost mild.
Siringo had pawned his pistol at the Rocky Mountain Pawn Shop
and had borrowed a pistol from a friend. He had received his wages
and was on his way to the pawn shop to redeem his pistol. Next door
to the shop a chemical factory had blown up, and it was reported
that a dead man was being brought out by the police and firemen.
A special policeman was placed in front of the pawn shop to protect
it. Siringo stepped up on the iron railing in order to see the dead
man as he was brought out. He writes:

Just then young Solomon told me to get down and move away from the
front of their shop. I told him to go to Hades or some other seaport. Then
the big double-jointed special policeman pulled me down and tore my coat

almost off. My gold-headed silk umbrella was broken all to pieces over his head and when he reached for his gun mine was pulled out of my hip pocket and pointed at his heart and the trigger was pulled. While using the umbrella on the fellow's head, other policemen rushed at me. Just as the trigger was pulled, a policeman by the name of Ball, threw both arms around me from the rear. His right hand grabbed the pistol and the hammer came down on his thumb instead of the cartridge, thus saving me the expense of a trip to the penitentiary, for had he been killed, it would have meant a trip "over the road." The sharp hammer had buried itself in his thumb, so I was told. I saw him many times afterwards, but never made myself known to him.[20]

Another example of understatement is in Siringo's account of his receiving a letter from his best girl friend, telling him that she had married another man. He quit his job immediately. He wanted to die, and so he resolved to go to the Black Hills, where, as a result of a gold rush, it was easy for a man to get killed. On his way, he went through Wichita, Kansas, and spent three days there, dead drunk. He ended up broke and rode out of town with no destination in view. "To tell the truth," he writes, "I was still somewhat rattled over my recent bad luck."[21]

Another time he roped a large steer, which jerked his horse over backwards on top of him. When the horse got up, Siringo became all wound up in the rope, so that he could not free himself. The pony was wild, and as the cowboy hung fast to his side with his head down, the steer, which was still fastened to the rope, was making every effort to gore him and the horse. Siringo's comment is, "I was certainly in a ticklish predicament that time."[22]

It is hard to separate Siringo's humor, either conscious or unconscious, from his use of the idiom of the cow country. Seldom is his humor as broad as that found in his preface to *A Texas Cow Boy*. He used the speech patterns and idiom of the West without discrimination. Some of the cowboy expressions, such as "guard" and "mount", he placed in quotation marks, showing that he knew that they were not standard. However, he used such expressions as "sore-head," "checked up" (meaning stopped), "muley" (meaning tenderfoot, also called "short-horn"), "locoed" (crazy), "grub" (food), "bug juice" (liquor), and "pard" without using quotation marks. He used many colorful, pithy expressions such as those in the following description of a very cold night which he spent after losing his blankets and equipment by fire:

I pitched camp about nine o'clock that night and played a single-handed game of freeze-out until morning, not having any matches to make a fire with.[23]

His description of a horse trade is slangy:

On arriving in Denton that time, a negro struck me for a horse swap right away. I got a three year old pony and six dollars in money for my mare; the pony suited just as well for a pack animal as the mare.[24]

He was fond of using the similes which were a part of the colorful language of the cow country; the following were gleaned from *A Texas Cow Boy*. Once, while he was razing a house, it fell on him and on a neighbor boy, who was asleep inside. Siringo said that the boy woke and "began squalling like a six month old calf being put through the process of branding." Leaving his favorite horse, Whiskey Pete, behind him was as bad as "having sixteen jaw-teeth pulled." Speaking of the good times he and a friend had at a line camp one winter, he wrote, "John and I built a small stone house on the head of the Bonetta Canyon and had a hog killing time all by ourselves." Siringo described the drinking spree which caused him to "swear off" drinking by stating that after the crowd came out of the saloon one of them was missing—a fellow just about Siringo's size. He was found lying hopelessly drunk under his horse, Whiskey Pete. His stomach felt "as though it were filled with scorpions, wild cats, and lizards." Once Siringo submitted a well-padded expense account to Beals, his employer. Every time Beals would come to one of the big bills, "he would grunt and crack about a forty-cent smile, but never kicked."

The effect of censorship and editing on Siringo's style is obvious. The most lively and interesting books are *A Texas Cow Boy* and *A Cowboy Detective*. In the early books he did not hesitate to relate incidents which put either him or one of his friends in an unfavorable light; often he exaggerated compromising situations as a humorous device. His language is more colorful than in the later volumes, although the later books are certainly not lacking in vitality. *A Texas Cow Boy* is fairly well organized; *A Lone Star Cowboy*, the first revision, shows the effect of such editing. The language is more subdued, and incidents that might reflect on the integrity of certain persons, including Siringo, are omitted. Some of the most interesting information of *A Texas Cow Boy* suffered in the editing of the later books. The revised material in *A Lone Star Cowboy* is usually in unnaturally short paragraphs because of the omission of some of the content; the added material is normally paragraphed. *Riata and Spurs*, the third revision, is much better organized, but not as lively. A comparison of the first paragraph of *A Texas Cow Boy* with the first paragraph of *Riata and Spurs* illustrates the toning down. In *A Texas Cow Boy* he writes,

It was a bright morning, on the 7th day of February, 1855, as near as I can remember, that your humble Servant came prancing into this wide and wicked world.

Riata and Spurs, though more subdued, still shows that Siringo was irrepressible:

I was born and brought up admidst wild, long-horn cattle and mustangs in the extreme southern part of the Lone Star State. I first saw the light of day and had my first warm meal on the seventh day of February, 1855, in the county of Matagorda, Texas.[25]

Numerous inconsistencies in spelling and capitalization found in *A Texas Cow Boy* were corrected in later publications. Chief among spelling errors· were *cow boy* (probably the original spelling), *mavrick* (for *maverick*) and *Cimeron* (for *Cimarron*). Most of the inconsistencies were in proper names, which he spelled phonetically; the word *maverick*, for example, was pronounced on the range as Siringo spelled it. His capitalization in the early books is very haphazard.

All of Siringo's books are readable. The early books, however, which are more uninhibited, are much more interesting to the modern reader. Their realism and authenticity as well as their rollicking style are more attractive to modern readers than they were when Siringo wrote.

IV   *Siringo's Place*

For thirty years, as I have read range histories, local histories of areas where Siringo worked, and general histories of the West and Southwest, I have routinely checked the indexes for mention of Siringo. Nearly all such histories, especially those written since J. Frank Dobie edited the 1950 edition of *A Texas Cow Boy*, have used Siringo's books as authentic history. A list of such books would be very long. My friends who have seen the Western movies of the last ten years say that Siringo is mentioned (or appears) in many of them. I have no desire, however, to do research in this area. At the time this is being written (summer 1976), a documentary film on the life of Siringo is being made for television at Yale University's new Media Design Studio, the first teleplay of a ten-film series entitled "Westering."[26]

These examples illustrate the growing interest in the life and works of an unusual American with an unusual ambition—to be in the middle of the numerous activities of a most interesting period in American history and to write about his experiences. I believe that what he set out to do, he did unusually well.

Notes and References

Chapter One

1. Charles A. Siringo, *A Texas Cowboy* (New York: William D. Sloane Associates, 1950), p. 7. Siringo's original spelling was "Cow Boy."
2. Charles D. Peavy, *Charles A. Siringo, A Texas Picaro* (Austin, Texas: Steck-Vaughn Company, 1967), (New York: Ginn and Company, 1931), p. 1.
3. Walter P. Webb, *The Great Plains* (New York: Ginn and Company, 1931), pp. 208 - 10.
4. *A Lone Star Cowboy* (Santa Fe, New Mexico: n.p., 1919), p. 1.
5. *A Texas Cowboy*, p. 8.
6. *Riata and Spurs* (Boston: Houghton Mifflin Company, 1927), p. 20.
7. *A Texas Cowboy*, p. 3.
8. "Charlie Siringo, Writer and Man," Introduction to *A Texas Cowboy*, pp. xiii - xiv.
9. *A Lone Star Cowboy*, pp. 229 - 30.
10. The real history of Billy the Kid, probably as much as will ever be known, may be found in Ramon F. Adams, *A Fitting Death for Billy the Kid* (Norman: University of Oklahoma Press, 1960) and in his fine bibliography, *Six-Guns and Saddle Leather* (Norman: University of Oklahoma Press, 1954).
11. See Charles D. Peavy, *Charles A. Siringo, A Texas Picaro*, pp. 22 - 23, and his introduction to the reprint of *Two Evil Isms* (Austin, Texas: Steck-Vaughn Company, 1967), pp. x - xi.
12. Charles A. Siringo, letters to Frank Caldwell (August 3, 1925, and September 14, 1927) and to Dr. E. A. Duncan (December 2, 1925), originals in the possession of Ben E. Pingenot, Eagle Pass, Texas.
13. *New York Times Book Review*, March 7, 1948, p. 8.
14. Chester Newton Hess, "Sagebrush Sleuth," *Cattleman* 41 (January 1955): 65.
15. O. W. Nolen, "Charley Siringo," *Cattleman* 38 (December 1951): 52.

Chapter Two

1. The best single source of information on the development of the Range Cattle Industry is Walter Prescott Webb's chapter entitled "The Cattle Kingdom," pp. 205 - 69 of *The Great Plains*. Attacked by lesser historians, Webb's thesis still stands. The best book on longhorns is J. Frank Dobie's *The Longhorns* (Boston: Little, Brown and Company, 1941). These

141

two sources alone provide a solid historical foundation for an understanding
of what happened in the development of the industry.

2. J. Frank Dobie, *The Longhorns*, pp. 27 - 28; *A Vaquero of the Brush
Country* (Dallas: Southwest Press, 1941), p. 46.

3. Mirabeau B., Lamar, *Papers*, ed. Charles Adams Gulick, Jr., and
others (Austin, Texas: A. C. Baldwin and Sons, 1921), III, pp. 107 - 10, 350,
424; IV, Part I, pp. 211 - 12; VI, pp. 99 - 100, 114 - 17, 136.

4. William A. Craigie and James R. Hulbert, eds., II, p. 658.

5. Dobie, *A Vaquero of the Brush Country*, p. 1.

6. *Riata and Spurs*, p. 120.

7. Ibid., p. 121.

8. Ibid., pp. 120 - 33.

9. *A Texas Cowboy*, p. 46.

10. Act of April 12, 1871, *The Penal Code of the State of Texas*, pp. 42 -
43.

11. *A Texas Cowboy*, p. 76.

12. *A Texas Cow Boy*, (1885), pp. 338 - 39.

13. Neil A. Clark, "Close Calls," *American Magazine* 107 (January
1929): 38.

14. *A Texas Cowboy*, p. 7.

15. *Riata and Spurs*, p. 121.

16. Ibid., p. 130; *A Texas Cowboy*, p. 16.

17. *Riata and Spurs*, p. 2.

18. Ibid., pp. 2, 131.

19. *A Texas Cowboy*, p. 43.

20. *The Longhorns*, pp. 46 - 48. The definitive discussion of the subject
is the chapter entitled "Mavericks and Maverickers," pp. 43 - 68. The first
footnote for the chapter gives an extensive list of sources.

21. *A Lone Star Cowboy*, pp. 1 - 2; *A Texas Cowboy*, pp. 17 - 18; *Riata
and Spurs*, p. 1.

22. *A Texas Cowboy*, pp. 18 - 42; *A Lone Star Cowboy*, pp. 2 - 10; *Riata
and Spurs*, pp. 2 - 7.

23. *A Texas Cowboy*, p. 42; *A Lone Star Cowboy*, pp. 10, 25; *Riata and
Spurs*, p. 7.

24. *A Texas Cowboy*, p. 44.

25. *Riata and Spurs*, p. 83.

26. George S. Saunders, "Shanghai Pierce," J. Marvin Hunter, ed., *Trail
Drivers of Texas* (Nashville, Tennessee: Cokesbury Press, 1925), pp. 923 -
924. A full study of Pierce is Chris Emmett's *Shanghai Pierce, A Fair
Likeness* (Norman: University of Oklahoma Press, 1953).

27. *Riata and Spurs*, pp. 8, 14, 53.

28. *A Texas Cowboy*, p. 44; *A Lone Star Cowboy*, pp. 11 - 12; *Riata and
Spurs*, pp. 7 - 8.

29. *A Texas Cowboy*, p. 44; *A Lone Star Cowboy*, p. 11; *Riata and
Spurs*, p. 8.

30. Philip Ashton Rollins, *The Cowboy* (New York: Charles Scribner's Sons, 1956), p. 109; *A Lone Star Cowboy*, p. 223.

31. *A Lone Star Cowboy*, p. 40.

32. *A Texas Cow Boy* (1886), pp. 337 - 38.

33. *A Texas Cowboy*, pp. 44 - 45; *A Lone Star Cowboy*, p. 12 - 13; *Riata and Spurs*, pp. 8 - 9.

34. *A Lone Star Cowboy*, p. 13; *Riata and Spurs*, p. 9.

35. *The Longhorns*, p. 213.

36. *A Texas Cowboy*, pp. 48 - 49.

37. *A Texas Cowboy*, pp. 45 - 46; *A Lone Star Cowboy*, p. 14; *Riata and Spurs*, p. 9.

38. *A Lone Star Cowboy*, p. 17; *Riata and Spurs*, p. 11.

39. *A Texas Cowboy*, pp. 51 - 52; *A Lone Star Cowboy*, pp. 16 - 20; *Riata and Spurs*, pp. 11 - 12.

40. *A Texas Cowboy*, p. 40; *A Lone Star Cowboy*, pp. 16 - 20; *Riata and Spurs*, pp. 10 - 12.

41. *A Texas Cowboy*, p. 52; *A Lone Star Cowboy*, p. 20; *Riata and Spurs*, p. 12.

42. *A Lone Star Cowboy*, pp. 23 - 24; *Riata and Spurs*, p. 14.

43. J. Frank Dobie, *A Vaquero of the Brush Country*, pp. 23 - 24.

44. *A Texas Cowboy*, pp. 56 - 57; *A Lone Star Cowboy*, pp. 23 - 24; *Riata and Spurs*, pp. 13 - 14.

45. *A Texas Cowboy*, pp. 55, 65 - 66; *Riata and Spurs*, pp. 14 - 15.

46. *A Texas Cowboy*, p. 72; *A Lone Star Cowboy*, pp. 30 - 31; *Riata and Spurs*, pp. 18 - 19.

47. *A Lone Star Cowboy*, pp. 25 - 26; *Riata and Spurs*, pp. 15 - 16.

Chapter Three

1. George W. Saunders, "A Log of the Trails," *Trail Drivers of Texas* (1925), p. 962. The 1925 edition multiplies these figures by ten, but the original edition, 1920, gave the smaller, more accurate figures.

2. J. Frank Dobie, *Guide to Life and Literature of the Southwest*, revised edition (Dallas: Southern Methodist University Press, 1952), p. 108.

3. Orlan Sawey, "The Cowboy Autobiography," dissertation, University of Texas, 1953.

4. For accounts of trail driving before 1967, see Douglas Branch, *The Cowboy and His Interpreters* (New York: D. Appleton and Company, 1926), pp. 6 - 7, and Wayne Gard, *The Chisholm Trail* (Norman: University of Oklahoma Press, 1954), pp. 20 - 56. For an account of McCoy's opening of the Abilene market, see Joseph G. McCoy's *Historic Sketches of the Cattle Trade of the West and Southwest* (Kansas City: Ramsey Millet and Hudson, 1874), and Gard, pp. 57 - 84, which also includes a complete history of Chisholm's involvement.

5. Walter Prescott Webb, *The Great Plains*, p. 216.

6. See Webb, *The Great Frontier*, pp. 180 - 202.

7. *A Lone Star Cowboy*, pp. 270 - 71.

8. *Riata and Spurs* (revised), pp. 254 - 55.

9. *A Lone Star Cowboy*, p. 18.

10. *Riata and Spurs* (revised), pp. 255 - 56.

11. Martha Burton, "The Removal of the Wichitas from Butler County, Kansas, to the Present Agency," *The Panhandle-Plains Historical Review* 4 (1931): 66 - 72; Rupert N. Richardson, *The Comanche Barrier to the South Plains Settlement* (Glendale: The Arthur H. Clark Company, 1933), p. 313.

12. "Origin and Close of the Old-Time Northern Trail," *The Trail Drivers of Texas* (1925), p. 20.

13. See Gard, pp. 77, 229.

14. *A Lone Star Cowboy*, p. 42; *Riata and Spurs* (revised), p. 26.

15. George W. Saunders, "A Log of the Trails"; C. H. Rust, "Location of the Old Chisholm Trail"; and Jack Potter, "Coming Up the Trail in 1882"; all in *The Trail Drivers of Texas* (1925), pp. 959 - 64, 37 - 41, 58 - 59.

16. *A Texas Cowboy*, pp. 76 ff., 120. For estimates of Siringo's height see Neil M. Clark, "Close Calls," *American Magazine* 107 (January 1929): 38; Eugene Manlove Rhodes, "He'll Make a Hand," *Sunset Magazine* 63 (June 1927): 23; Chester Newton Hess, "Sagebrush Sleuth," *Cattleman* 41 (January 1955): 36.

17. *A Texas Cowboy*, pp. 58 - 61.

18. Ibid., pp. 76 - 77; *A Lone Star Cowboy*, pp. 37 - 40; *Riata and Spurs*, pp. 23 - 25.

19. *A Lone Star Cowboy*, pp. 37 - 42; *Riata and Spurs*, pp. 21 - 26.

20. *A Lone Star Cowboy*, pp. 43 - 44.

21. Ibid., p. 44. Siringo gave the words for the first three songs in his list in *The Song Companion to A Lone Star Cowboy*. Either his memory was faulty, or the "such as" meant he was not trying to give specific titles for that occasion, because Sam Bass was still alive in 1876. The ballad was not composed until after Bass's death in 1878.

22. *A Lone Star Cowboy*, pp. 44 - 47.

23. E. C. Abbott and Helena Huntington Smith, *We Pointed Them North* (New York: Farrar and Rinehart, 1939), p. 4.

24. *A Texas Cowboy*, p. 77.

25. *A Lone Star Cowboy*, p. 88; *Riata and Spurs*, p. 27.

26. *A Texas Cowboy*, pp. 77 - 79; *A Lone Star Cowboy*, pp. 47 - 51; *Riata and Spurs*, pp. 27 - 29.

27. *A Texas Cowboy*, pp. 80 - 81; *A Lone Star Cowboy*, p. 52; *Riata and Spurs*, p. 29.

28. *A Texas Cowboy*, p. 81.

29. *A Lone Star Cowboy*, p. 52; *Riata and Spurs*, p. 30.

30. Neil M. Clark, "Close Calls," *American Magazine* 107 (January 1929): 38.

31. *A Lone Star Cowboy,* pp. 52 - 53; *Riata and Spurs,* pp. 30 - 31.

32. *A Texas Cowboy,* pp. 81 - 87; *A Lone Star Cowboy,* pp. 55 - 56; *Riata and Spurs,* pp. 31 - 32.

33. *A Texas Cowboy,* pp. 38 - 92; *A Lone Star Cowboy,* pp. 56 - 61; Riata and Spurs, pp. 32 - 35.

34. *A Texas Cowboy,* pp. 92 - 93; *A Lone Star Cowboy,* pp. 63 - 65; *Riata and Spurs,* pp. 35 - 37.

35. *A Lone Star Cowboy,* pp. 64 - 65.

Chapter Four

1. For geographical data in this chapter I am indebted to the *Dallas Morning News Texas Almanac,* 1976 - 1977, which invariably tells one more than he wants to know about any Texas subject.

2. Rupert Norval Richardson, *The Comanche Barrier to North Plains Settlement* (see p. 242), pp. 317 - 97. This is one of many histories of the subjugation of the Plains Indians.

3. Laura V. Hamner, *Short Grass & Longhorns,* p. 4.

4. Ibid., pp. 44 - 46.

5. *A Texas Cowboy,* p. 93.

6. Ibid., pp. 93 - 98; *A Lone Star Cowboy,* pp. 71 - 72; *Riata and Spurs,* pp. 39 - 41.

7. *A Lone Star Cowboy,* pp. 37 - 66.

8. *A Texas Cowboy,* pp. 94 - 96; *A Lone Star Cowboy,* pp. 94 - 96; *Riata and Spurs,* p. 39.

9. *A Texas Cowboy,* pp. 100 - 101; *A Lone Star Cowboy,* pp. 81 - 82; *Riata and Spurs,* pp. 45 - 46.

10. *A Lone Star Cowboy,* p. 166.

11. Ibid., pp. 79 - 80, 93; *Riata and Spurs,* pp. 44, 53, 67 - 68.

12. Laura Hamner, *Short Grass & Longhorns* (Norman: University of Oklahoma Press, 1943), pp. 90 - 91.

13. *A Texas Cowboy,* pp. 99 - 100, 103 - 105; *A Lone Star Cowboy,* pp. 89, 91, 94; *Riata and Spurs,* pp. 51 - 54.

14. *A Lone Star Cowboy,* pp. 91 - 92; *Riata and Spurs,* pp. 52 - 53.

15. *A Texas Cowboy,* pp. 105 - 106; *A Lone Star Cowboy,* pp. 97 - 98; *Riata and Spurs,* p. 57.

16. *A Texas Cowboy,* pp. 106 - 10; *A Lone Star Cowboy,* pp. 98 - 107; *Riata and Spurs,* pp. 57 - 63.

17. *A Texas Cowboy,* pp. 110 - 24; *A Lone Star Cowboy,* pp. 111 - 23; *Riata and Spurs,* pp. 69 - 73.

Chapter Five

1. Pat F. Garrett, *Authentic Life of Billy the Kid* (New York: Funk & Wagnalls Company, 1958), p. 3, and Miguel A. Otero, *The Real Billy the*

Kid, with New Light on the Lincoln County War (New York: Rufus Rockwell Wilson, Inc., 1936), p. 3.

2. See note 10, Chapter 1, this book.

3. Neil M. Clark, "Close Calls," *American Magazine* 108 (January 1929): 38 - 39.

4. *Riata and Spurs*, pp. 89 - 90.

5. See *Riata and Spurs*, facing p. 258, and James S. Guyer, *Pioneer Life in Texas* (Brownwood, Texas: James S. Guyer, 1938), pp. 104, 114.

6. Someone has suggested that Siringo's calling the Kid's girl friend at Fort Sumner "Dulcinea del Tobosco" indicates that the novel was *Don Quixote*. Siringo, the Kid, and a finely bound novel, whether *Don Quixote* or not—these are not the usual elements of the Western bad-man story.

7. *A Texas Cowboy*, p. 110; *A Lone Star Cowboy*, pp. 109 - 10; *Riata and Spurs*, pp. 63 - 64.

8. *History of "Billy the Kid,"* p. 3.

9. *A Fitting Death for Billy the Kid*, p. 167 et passim.

10. *A Texas Cowboy*, p. 125.

11. Ibid., pp. 125 - 28; *A Lone Star Cowboy*, pp. 133 - 34; *Riata and Spurs*, pp. 75 - 76.

12. *A Texas Cowboy*, pp. 127 - 30; *A Lone Star Cowboy*, p. 134; *Riata and Spurs*, p. 76.

13. J. Evetts Haley, "Jim East, Trail Hand and Cowboy," *Panhandle-Plains Historical Review* 4 (1931): 52 - 55.

14. *History of "Billy the Kid,"* p. 97.

15. *Authentic Life of Billy the Kid*, pp. 157 - 58.

16. *A Texas Cowboy*, pp. 130 - 42; *A Lone Star Cowboy*, pp. 135 - 56; *Riata and Spurs*, pp. 66 - 83.

17. *A Texas Cowboy*, pp. 142 - 59; *A Lone Star Cowboy*, pp. 146 - 65; *Riata and Spurs*, pp. 83 - 91.

18. *A Texas Cowboy*, pp. 160 - 67, 178 - 92; *A Lone Star Cowboy*, pp. 165 - 203; *Riata and Spurs*, pp. 92 - 110.

Chapter Six

1. Laura V. Hamner, *Short Grass & Longhorns*, p. 4.

2. J. Evetts Haley, *Charles Goodnight* (Boston: Houghton Mifflin Company, 1936), pp. 302 - 305.

3. *A Lone Star Cowboy*, pp. 166 - 67; *Riata and Spurs*, pp. 92 - 93.

4. Haley, pp. 384 ff.

5. Ibid., pp. 321 - 22.

6. *A Texas Cowboy*, pp. 196 - 98; *A Lone Star Cowboy*, pp. 205 - 14; *Riata and Spurs*, pp. 111 - 15.

7. See Dobie's Preface to *A Texas Cowboy*, pp. x - xi.

8. *A Texas Cow Boy* (1886), p. 317. The edition used in this discussion

is one printed by Rand McNally and Company, Chicago, no date. See pp. xxxvii - xxxviii of Dobie's 1950 edition for full bibliographical data.

9. Ibid., pp. 317 - 18.
10. Ibid., pp. 318 - 45.
11. Ibid., p. 318.
12. Ibid., p. 321.
13. Ibid., p. 323.
14. Ibid., p. 325.
15. Ibid., pp. 341 - 42.
16. Ibid., pp. 337 - 39.
17. Ibid., p. 338.
18. Ibid., p. 340.
19. Ibid., pp. 326 - 36.
20. Ibid., pp. 346 - 47.
21. *Riata and Spurs* (revised), p. 132.
22. Ibid., pp. 260 - 61.

Chapter Seven

1. *Riata and Spurs*, p. 119.
2. Ibid., p. 118.
3. Ibid., pp. 116 - 18.
4. Ibid., p. 118. The description of the tournament is based on my own observation.
5. Charles D. Peavy, Introduction to *Two Evil Isms* (Austin, Texas: Steck-Vaughn Company, 1967), pp. iv - v. Siringo's signed report, attached to a Houghton Mifflin interoffice memorandum dated January 18, 1927; letter from Pinkerton lawyer to Houghton Mifflin Company, May 27, 1927.
6. *A Cowboy Detective*, p. 5.
7. James D. Horan, *The Pinkertons: The Detective Dynasty That Made History* (New York: Crown Publishers, 1967), p. 458.
8. See footnote 5, above.
9. Interoffice memorandum, Houghton Mifflin Company, March 2, 1926.
10. Interoffice memoranda, Houghton Mifflin Company, April 26, 1926; May 4, 1926; June 15, 1926; July 1, 1926; September 27, 1926; and October 1, 1926.
11. Decree of the Superior Court of Cook County, Illinois, General Number 277903, Term Number 5868, December 12, 1911, *Pinkerton's National Detective Agency* v. *Charles A. Siringo and W. B. Conkey Company*.
12. The memoranda and letters which follow are from the Houghton Mifflin file and are identified only by dates. I think that the names of those involved are not important to the account.

148 CHARLES A. SIRINGO

13. James D. Horan, *Desperate Men* (New York: G. P. Putnam's Sons, 1949), p. vii.

14. *A Cowboy Detective*, p. 10.

15. Siringo's letters of July 13, 1915, in Peavy's introduction to *Two Evil Isms* (1967), pp. viii - x.

16. *A Cowboy Detective*, pp. 13 - 15; *Riata and Spurs*, pp. 121 - 23. Sources of the account of Siringo's years as a Pinkerton detective will be these two books and *Two Evil Isms;* the original edition of *Riata and Spurs* will be used. The basic source will be *A Cowboy Detective*, which is the most detailed, with *Riata and Spurs* and *Two Evil Isms* being used for names, since the names in *A Cowboy Detective* are fictitious. When the books do not agree in details, the disagreements will be noted.

17. *A Cowboy Detective*, pp. 12 - 31; *Riata and Spurs*, pp. 120 - 24; *Two Evil Isms*, pp. 1 - 2.

Chapter Eight

1. *Two Evil Isms*, pp. 2 - 4.

2. Ibid., pp. 4 - 5.

3. A good account of this event is Henry David, *The History of the Haymarket Affair* (New York: Russell and Russell, 1958). There are many unanswered questions about what really happened, some of which will never be answered. David's excellent bibliography includes Siringo's *Two Evil Isms*.

4. This summary is of materials from Ray Ginger's *Altgeld's America: The Lincoln Ideal versus Changing Realities* (New York: Funk & Wagnalls Company, 1958), pp. 44 - 49. Ginger's account seems to me to be the most succinct and accurate. *Riata and Spurs*, pp. 120 - 21; *Two Evil Isms*, pp. 1 - 2.

5. *A Cowboy Detective*, pp. 11 - 12; *Riata and Spurs*, pp. 119 - 21.

6. *A Cowboy Detective*, p. 21; *Riata and Spurs*, pp. 124 - 25; *Two Evil Isms*, p. 5.

7. *A Cowboy Detective*, pp. 21 - 22; *Riata and Spurs*, pp. 124 - 26; *Two Evil Isms*, pp. 5 - 7. For an account of Schnaubelt's later years, see David, *The History of the Haymarket Affair*, pp. 508 - 14.

8. *A Cowboy Detective*, p. 21; *Riata and Spurs*, p. 126; *Two Evil Isms*, p. 6.

9. David, pp. 489 - 503; Ginger, pp. 78 - 88.

10. *A Cowboy Detective*, pp. 22 - 23.

11. David, p. 341.

12. *A Cowboy Detective*, p. 23; *Two Evil Isms*, p. 8.

13. *A Cowboy Detective*, p. 24.

14. See frontispiece, *Riata and Spurs*, and a two-page spread between pp. 348 and 349 of *A Cowboy Detective*.

15. The account of the Archuleta County dispute is taken from *A Cow-*

boy Detective, pp. 25 - 35; *Riata and Spurs*, pp. 127 - 28; and *Two Evil Isms*, pp. 11 - 12.

16. *Two Evil Isms*, p. 11.

17. Frank C. Pierce, *A Brief History of the Lower Rio Grande Valley* (Menesca, Wisconsin: George Banta Publishing Company, 1917), pp. 118 - 20; a full account can be found in Frank Dugan, "A Gift of the Rio Grande: The Story of Hidalgo County," 1952, unpublished manuscript, pp. 376 - 417.

18. *A Cowboy Detective*, p. 27.

19. Ibid., p. 33.

20. Mary Hallock Foote, *Coeur d'Alene* (Boston: Houghton Mifflin Company, 1894), p. 44; John Hays Hammond, "Strong Men of the West," *Scribner's Magazine* 77 (February 1925): 121 - 25; William T. Stoll, *Silver Strike*, pp. 183 - 248. A secondary account sympathetic to the miners and a list of sources may be found in Richard E. Lingenfelter, *The Hardrock Miners: A History of the Mining Labor Movement in the American West, 1863 - 1893* (Berkeley: University of California Press, 1974), pp. 197 - 218, 247 - 48.

21. *Two Evil Isms*, p. 36. The direct quotation of McParland's charge in *A Cowboy Detective*, p. 136, only approximates what is quoted here.

22. *Two Evil Isms*, p. 37.

23. The summary which follows is from *A Cowboy Detective*, pp. 135 - 91; *Riata and Spurs*, pp. 158 - 83; *Two Evil Isms*, pp. 36 - 42.

24. Hammond, pp. 123 - 25.

25. *A Cowboy Detective*, p. 162.

26. Lingenfelter, p. 215.

27. *A Cowboy Detective*, pp. 510 - 26; *Riata and Spurs*, pp. 257 - 62; *Two Evil Isms*, pp. 94 - 96. The account of Siringo's involvement, which follows, is based on these sources.

28. Marian C. McKenna, *Borah* (Ann Arbor: University of Michigan Press, 1961), pp. 48 - 50.

Chapter Nine

1. The summary of this chase is from *A Cowboy Detective*, pp. 51 - 65; *Riata and Spurs*, pp. 131 - 32.

2. The account of the death and funeral, in *A Cowboy Detective*, pp. 61 - 62, is a well-written comic scene.

3. William French, *Some Recollections of a Western Rancher, New Mexico, 1883 - 1889* (London: Methuen and Company, 1927), pp. 251 - 83.

4. John H. (Jack) Culley, *Cattle, Horses and Men of the Western Range* (Los Angeles: Ward Ritchie Press, 1940), p. 34.

5. James D. Horan, *Desperate Men*, pp. 183 - 93.

6. Informative accounts of the Wild Bunch's confusing history are two of Horan's books, *Desperate Men*, pp. 175 - 291, and *The Pinkertons*, pp.

283 - 89. James D. Horan's *The Wild Bunch*, published in 1958 by Signet Books, was produced for popular consumption. Although Horan insists that the book is accurate, based on primary sources, he does not tell us what those sources were. *The Wild Bunch* follows the traditional accounts, including the story of the death of Cassidy and the Sundance Kid in Bolivia. The book is a sloppy, hurried product, replete with errors in areas where Horan should know better; an example is his calling J. B. McParland, superintendent of the Denver Pinkerton office, McPharland.

Charles Kelly's *The Outlaw Trail: A History of Butch Cassidy and His Wild Bunch*, first published in 1938 and revised in 1959, may have been one of Horan's sources. Kelly also assures us that his sources are reliable, but he does not tell us what they were. Long conversations, reported verbatim, a device of the fictional biographer, make the account suspect.

7. The list was compiled from two lists by Horan: *Desperate Men*, pp. 208 - 209, and *The Pinkertons*, pp. 383 - 84.

8. Horan, *Desperate Men*, pp. 242 - 43.

9. The summary which follows is from *A Cowboy Detective*, pp. 305 - 80, and *Riata and Spurs*, pp. 209 - 51.

10. *Desperate Men*, pp. 209 - 10.

11. *A Cowboy Detective*, p. 312.

12. Horan, *The Pinkertons*, p. 388.

13. Ibid., p. 387; *Desperate Men*, pp. 287 - 90. See *A Lone Star Cowboy*, pp. 235 - 44, and *Riata and Spurs*, pp. 267 - 68.

14. *A Cowboy Detective*, pp. 395 - 449. The ballad stanza appears on page 437.

Chapter Ten

1. *A Cowboy Detective*, pp. 133 - 34.

2. Ibid., p. 116.

3. *Riata and Spurs* (revised), p. 263.

4. A more complete discussion of Siringo's Santa Fe years can be found in Ben E. Pingenot's "Charlie Siringo, New Mexico's Lone Star Cowboy," *Cattleman* 63 (November 1976): 56 - 57, 122 - 28.

5. *Riata and Spurs* (revised), pp. 263 - 74.

6. Siringo, letters to Frank Caldwell, August 3, 1925, and September 14, 1927, originals in collection of Ben E. Pingenot, Eagle Pass, Texas; O. W. Nolen, "Charley Siringo, Old-Time Cowboy Rancher, Detective, and Author," *Cattleman* 38 (December 1951): 54, 56; Eugene Manlove Rhodes, "He'll Make a Hand," *Sunset Magazine* 58 (June 1927): 23, 89 - 91; Neil M. Clark, "Close Calls: an Interview with Charles A. Siringo," *American Magazine* 107 (January 1929): 38 - 39, 129 - 31; J. Evetts Haley, "Charles A. Siringo," *Dictionary of American Biography*, XVII, 191 - 92. Unreliable memory and sloppy research perhaps should remain unrecorded, but in 1947 I read somewhere that Siringo wrote scenarios for William S. Hart

movies and played bit parts in the same movies. I have been unable to document this information.

7. "Close Calls," *American Magazine* 107 (January 1929): 38.

8. *Guide to Life and Literature of the Southwest*, p. 119.

9. See Joe B. Frantz and Julian Ernest Choate, Jr., *The American Cowboy: The Myth and the Reality* (Norman: University of Oklahoma Press, 1955), pp. 104 ff.

10. Jim Tully, review in *New York World*, June 5, 1927, p. 7.

11. B. W. Smith, Jr., review in *New York Post Literary Review*, May 9, 1927, p. 3.

12. William Rose Benet, "Quick on the Draw," *Saturday Review of Literature* 4 (August 27, 1927): 69 - 70.

13. Owen P. White, "Six Shooters, Cinch Rings, Longhorns and Saloons," *The New York Times Book Review*, May 3, 1927, p. 6.

14. *American Review of Reviews* 75 (June 1927): 668.

15. J. Frank Dobie, "Old Charlie," *Nation* 125 (July 13, 1927): 4.

16. Walter Prescott Webb, "Charlie Siringo Tells the Story of Thrilling Life on the Frontier," *Dallas Morning News*, May 8, 1927, Section 3, p. 3.

17. *A Texas Cowboy*, pp. 195 - 98.

18. *Riata and Spurs*, p. 18.

19. *A Cowboy Detective*, pp. 17 - 18.

20. Ibid., pp. 98 - 99.

21. *A Texas Cowboy*, pp. 82 - 83.

22. Ibid., p 49.

23. Ibid., p. 89.

24. Ibid., p. 116.

25. Ibid., p. 7; *Riata and Spurs*, p. 1.

26. Les Brown, "Yale Professor to Make TV Westerns," *Corpus Christi Caller-Times*, TV Section, April 11, 1976, p. 14. A syndicated column of the *New York Times* News Service.

Selected Bibliography

This bibliography consists of books by Siringo, works about him, works in which he is discussed, and books used as background for various phases of his life. It does not include the many rangeland histories which mention him and which have used his works as a source, nor does it include several critical works which give a brief evaluation of his writing.

PRIMARY SOURCES

The annotations consist mainly of Siringo's lengthy title pages.

A Cowboy Detective. A True Story of Twenty-Two Years with a World-Famous Detective Agency. Giving Inside Facts of the Bloody Coeur d'Alene Labor Riots, and the many Ups and Downs of the Author, throughout the United States, Alaska, British Columbia, and Mexico. Also Exciting Scenes among the Moonshiners of Kentucky and Virgina. By Charles A. Siringo, Author of "A Texas Cowboy." Chicago: W. B. Conkey Company, 1912. Paperback edition, in two volumes, by J. S. Ogilvie Publishing Company, 57 Rose Street, New York, as Numbers 127 and 128 in the Railroad Series. Volume I, which was entitled *A Cowboy Detective*, included the original book through p. 246; Volume II, entitled *Further Adventures of a Cowboy Detective*, included pp. 247 - 519.

History of "Billy the Kid." The true life of the most daring young outlaw of the age. He was the leading spirit in the bloody Lincoln County, New Mexico, war. When a bullet from Sheriff Pat Garrett's [sic] pistol pierced his breast he was only twenty-one years of age, and had killed twenty-one men, not counting Indians. His six years of daring outlawry has never been equalled in the annals of criminal history. By Chas. A. Siringo. Author of: "Fifteen Years on the Hurricane Deck of a Spanish Pony," "A Cowboy Detective," and "A Lone Star Cowboy." Sante Fe, New Mexico, 1920. A facsimile reproduction, with an introduction by Charles D. Peavy, was published in 1967 by Steck-Vaughn Company, Austin, Texas.

A Lone Star Cowboy. Being fifty years experience in the saddle as Cowboy, Detective, and New Mexico Ranger, on every cow trail in the wooly [sic] old west. Also the doings of some "bad" cowboys, such as "Billy the Kid," Wess Harding [sic] and "Kid Curry." By Chas. A. Siringo. Author of: "Fifteen Years on the Hurricane Deck of a Spanish Pony" and "A Cowboy Detective." Santa Fe, New Mexico, 1919.

Riata and Spurs. The Story of a Lifetime spent in the Saddle as Cowboy and Detective. By Charles A. Siringo. With an Introduction by Gifford Pinchot. And with illustrations. Boston and New York: Houghton Mifflin Company, 1927. The second and subsequent printings, one dated 1931, substitute "Ranger" for "Detective" in the subtitle. Pages 120 - 276 in the first printing deal mainly with Siringo's experiences as a Pinkerton detective. Pages 120 - 261 of the revised printing deal mainly with various bad men of the West.

A Song Companion to A Lone Star Cowboy. Santa Fe, New Mexico, 1920. A slight collection of forty-two pages. Replica edition by Norwood Editions, 1975.

A Texas Cow Boy or, Fifteen Years on the Hurricane Deck of a Spanish Pony. Taken from real life, by Chas. A. Siringo, an Old Stove-up "Cow Puncher" Who Has Spent Nearly Twenty Years on the Great Western Cattle Ranges. Chicago: M. Umbdenstock and Co., Publishers, 1885. Second edition, 1886. Same title page, but shows Siringo & Dobson, Publishers, Chicago. Contains "Addenda," pp. 317 - 57. This is the edition which was reprinted an indeterminate number of times by Rand McNally and Company, Chicago and New York, and the Eagle Publishing Company, which, Dobie says, "seems to have been a subsidiary" of Rand McNally. Many of the printings were in paperback. A cheaper paperback edition was printed in 1914 by J. S. Ogilvie Publishing Company, New York, and kept in print until 1926. See Dobie, next list, for later reprints.

Two Evil Isms: Pinkertonism and Anarchism. By a Cowboy Detective Who Knows, as He Spent Twenty-Two Years in the Inner Circle of Pinkerton's National Detective Agency. By Charles A. Siringo, Author of "A Texas Cowboy" and "A Cowboy Detective." Chicago: Charles A. Siringo, Publisher, 1915. A facsimile edition, with an introduction by Charles D. Peavy, was published by Steck-Vaughn Company, Austin, Texas, in 1967.

SECONDARY SOURCES

1. Works Dealing Directly and Extensively with Siringo.

ADAMS, CLARENCE SIRINGO. "Fair Trial at Encino," *True West* 5 (March-April 1966): 32 - 33, 50 - 51. Adams was not kin to Siringo: he was named for him.

APPLEMAN, ROY E. *Charlie Siringo, Cowboy Detective*. Washington, D.C.: Potomac Corral, The Westerners, 1968. Pamphlet. Rehash.

BENET, WILLIAM ROSE. "Quick on the Draw," *Saturday Review of Literature* 4 (August 27, 1927): 69 - 70. Review of *Riata and Spurs*.

BRANCH, DOUGLAS. *The Cowboy and His Interpreters*. New York: D. Appleton and Company, 1926. Early and excellent account of cowboy literature; good on Siringo.

BROWN, JOHN A. *Charles A. Siringo*. Chicago: Brand Book, Chicago Corral, 1960, Vol. 16, No. 12. Slight Pamphlet.

BROWN, LES. "Yale Professor to Make TV Westerns," *Corpus Christi Caller-Times* TV Section, April 11, 1976, p. 14. Account of movie made on Siringo.

CLARK, NEIL M. "Close Calls: an Interview with Charles A. Siringo," *American Magazine* 107 (January 1929): 38 - 39, 130 - 31. Probably Siringo's last interview.

DOBIE, J. FRANK. "Charlie Siringo, Writer and Man," Introduction to *A Texas Cowboy*. New York: William Sloane Associates, 1950. Reprinted by University of Nebraska Press, 1966 and 1975.

————. "Old Charlie," *Nation* 125 (July 13, 1927): 41. Review of *Riata and Spurs*.

HALEY, J. EVETTS. "Charles A. Siringo," *Dictionary of American Biography*, XVII, 191 - 92. Contains bibliography.

HAMMOND, JOHN HAYS. "Strong Men of the West," *Scribner's Magazine* 77 (February and March 1925): 115 - 25, 246 - 56. Siringo in Idaho.

HESS, CHESTER NEWTON. "Sagebrush Sleuth," *Cattleman* 41 (January 1955): 36 - 37, 64 - 82. General rehash.

NOLEN, O. W. "Charley Siringo, Old-Time Cowboy, Rancher, Detective, and Author," *Cattleman* 38 (December 1951): 50 - 56. Some new information.

PEAVY, CHARLES D. *Charles A. Siringo: A Texas Picaro*. Austin, Texas: Steck-Vaughn Company, 1967. Pamphlet, Southwest Writers Series, No. 3. Siringo would laugh at the title.

————. Introduction to *History of "Billy the Kid."* Austin, Texas: Steck-Vaughn Company, 1967.

————. Introduction to *Two Evil Isms: Pinkertonism and Anarchism*. Austin, Texas: Steck-Vaughn Company, 1967.

PINGENOT, BEN E. "Charlie Siringo: New Mexico's Lone Star Cowboy," *Cattleman* 63 (November 1976): 56 - 57, 122 - 28. Siringo in Santa Fe.

Review of *Riata and Spurs*, *American Review of Reviews* 75 (June 1927): 668.

RHODES, EUGENE MANLOVE. "He'll Make a Hand," *Sunset Magazine* 63 (June 1927): 23, 89 - 91. Late interview.

SAWEY, ORLAN. "Charlie Siringo, Reluctant Propagandist," *Western American Literature* 7 (Fall 1972): 203 - 10. Siringo's "Addenda" to the second edition of *A Texas Cowboy*.

————. "Charles A. Siringo, Cowboy Chronicler," Master's Thesis, University of Texas, 1947. Siringo's cowboy life.

————. "The Cowboy Autobiography," Dissertation, University of Texas, 1953. History of ideas, open-range cowboy.

SMITH, B. W., JR. Review of *Riata and Spurs*, *New York Post Literary Review*, May 8, 1927, p. 3. Contemporary review.

THORP, RAYMOND W. "Cowboy Charley Siringo," *True West* 12 (January-February 1965): 32 - 33, 59 - 62. Imaginative.

TULLY, JIM. Review of *Riata and Spurs, New York World*, June 5, 1927, p. 7. Contemporary review.

WEBB, WALTER PRESCOTT. "Charlie Siringo Tells the Story of Thrilling Life on the Frontier," *Dallas Morning News*, May 8, 1927, Section 3, p. 3. A historian reviews the literary aspects of *Riata and Spurs*.

WHITE, OWEN P. "Six Shooters, Cinch Rings, Longhorns and Saloons," *New York Times Book Review*, May 9, 1927, p. 6. The title reflects more White than Siringo.

2. Works Referred to or Used as Background Material.

ABBOTT, E. C. ("Teddy Blue"), and SMITH, HELENA HUNTINGTON. *We Pointed Them North*. New York: Farrar and Rinehart, 1939. Rollicking rangeland reminiscences.

ADAMS, RAMON, F. *A Fitting Death for Billy the Kid*. Norman: University of Oklahoma Press, 1960. Iconoclastic account, with much new information.

———. *Six Guns and Saddle Leather: A Bibliography of Books and Pamphlets on Western Outlaws and Gunmen*. Norman: University of Oklahoma Press, 1954. Much on Billy the Kid.

BETENSON, LULA PARKER, as told to DORA FLACK. *Butch Cassidy, My Brother*. Provo: Brigham Young University, 1975. Aged sister's account of Butch's past, including "return."

BURTON, MARTHA. "The Removal of the Wichitas from Butler County, Kansas, to the Present Agency," *Panhandle-Plains Historical Review* 4 (1931): 66 - 72. Indian removal.

CRAIGIE, WILLIAM A., and HULBERT, JAMES R., eds. *A Dictionary of American English*. Chicago: University of Chicago Press, 1940. Historical approach; origin of word "cowboy."

CULLEY, JOHN H. (JACK). *Cattle, Horses and Men of the Western Range*. Los Angeles: Ward Ritchie Press, 1940. Englishman's analysis of cowboy nature.

DAVID, HENRY. *The History of the Haymarket Affair*. New York: Russell & Russell, 1936, 1958. Good history.

DOBIE, J. FRANK. *Guide to Life and Literature of the Southwest*. Dallas: Southern Methodist University Press, 1952. Basic, annotated bibliography.

———. *The Longhorns*. Boston: Little, Brown and Company, 1941. Rangeland history and folklore.

———. *A Vaquero of the Brush Country*. Dallas: Southwest Press, 1941. "Autobiography" of cowboy John Young; good Brush Country history—Dobie's, not Young's.

DUGAN, FRANK. "A Gift of the Rio Grande: the Story of Hidalgo County," 1952. County History; unpublished manuscript, unfortunately.

EMMETT, CHRIS. *Shanghai Pierce, A Fair Likeness*. Norman: University of Oklahoma Press, 1953. Good biography.

FOOTE, MARY HALLOCK. *Coeur d'Alene*. Boston: Hougton Mifflin Company, 1894. The big silver strike; the work of a Pinkerton detective (based on Siringo).

FRANTZ, JOE B., and CHOATE, JULIAN ERNEST, JR. *The American Cowboy: The Myth and the Reality*. Norman: University of Oklahoma Press, 1955. The "reality" is often myth.

FRENCH, WILLIAM. *Some Recollections of a Western Ranchman*. London: Methuen and Company, 1927. The Wild Bunch as cowboys.

GARD, WAYNE. *The Chisholm Trail*. Norman: University of Oklahoma Press, 1954. Good; based mainly on newspaper accounts.

GARRETT, PAT F. *Authentic Life of Billy the Kid*, Maurice Garland Fulton, ed. New York: Funk & Wagnalls Company, 1958. The legend maker, written by Ash Upson.

GINGER, RAY. *Altgeld's America: The Lincoln Ideal versus Changing Realities*. New York: Funk & Wagnalls Company, 1958. Aftermath of the Haymarket riots.

GUYER, JAMES, S. *Pioneer Life in Texas*. Brownwood, Texas: James Guyer, 1938. Possibly confused Siringo and Billy the Kid.

HALEY, J. EVETTS. *Charles Goodnight: Cowman and Plainsman*. Boston: Houghton Mifflin Company, 1936. Panhandle history.

————. "Jim East, Trail Hand and Cowboy," *Panhandle-Plains Historical Review* 4 (1931): 52 - 55. East chased Billy the Kid.

HAMNER, LAURA V. *Short Grass & Longhorns*. Norman: University of Oklahoma Press, 1943. Ranching in the Panhandle.

HORAN, JAMES D. *Desperate Men: Revelations from the Sealed Pinkerton Files*. New York: G. P. Putnam's Sons, 1949. Not all the files were unsealed.

————. *The Pinkertons: The Detective Dynasty that Made History*. New York: Crown Publishers, 1967. Authorized, King Robert version.

————. *The Wild Bunch*. New York: Signet Books, 1958. Popular history.

HUNTER, J. MARVIN, ed. *The Trail Drivers of Texas*, Second Edition. Nashville: Cokesbury Press, 1925. Basic source on the cattle trails and trail driving.

KELLY, CHARLES. *The Outlaw Trail: A History of Butch Cassidy and the Wild Bunch*. New York: Bonanza Books, 1959. Popular history.

LAMAR, MIRABEAU B. *Papers*, ed. Charles Adams Gulick and others. Austin: A. C. Baldwin and Sons, 1921. Cites early use of the word "cowboy."

LINGENFELTER, RICHARD E. *The Hardrock Miners: A History of the Mining Labor Movement in the American West, 1863 - 1893*. Berkeley: University of California Press, 1974. Source of information on the Coeur d'Alene troubles.

McCOY, JOSEPH G. *Historic Sketches of the Cattle Trade of the West and*

Southwest. Kansas City: Ramsey, Millet, and Hudson, 1874. Basic work on Abilene and the Chisholm Trail.

McKENNA, MARIAN C. *Borah*. Ann Arbor: University of Michigan Press, 1961. Good account of the Haywood trial.

OTERO, MIGUEL ANTONIO. *The Real Billy the Kid, with New Light on the Lincoln County War*. New York: Rufus Rockwell Wilson, Inc., 1936. New Mexico governor breaks trails that lead nowhere.

The Penal Code of Texas, 1879. Galveston: H. H. Belo and Company, 1879. Contains Texas gun law.

PIERCE, FRANK. *A Brief History of the Lower Rio Grande Valley*. Menesca, Wisconsin: George Banta Publishing Company, 1917. "Anarchy" in Texas.

POINTER, LARRY. *In Search of Butch Cassidy*. Norman: University of Oklahoma Press, 1977. Did he find him?

RICHARDSON, RUPERT NORVAL. *The Comanche Barrier to the South Plains Settlement*. Glendale: Arthur H. Clark Company, 1933. Basic work on Indian removal.

ROLLINS, PHILIP ASHTON. *The Cowboy*. New York: Charles Scribner's Sons, 1936. Description of cowboy life.

STOLL, WILLIAM T., as told to H. W. WHICHER. *Silver Strike: The True Story of Silver Mining in the Coeur d'Alenes*. Boston: Little, Brown and Company, 1932. Stoll, a lawyer and mine owner, corroborates Siringo's account.

WEBB, WALTER PRESCOTT. *The Great Frontier*. Boston: Houghton Mifflin Company, 1952. The Great Frontier is America; the metropolis is Europe.

_____. *The Great Plains*. New York: Ginn and Company, 1931. Basic historical interpretation of the Cattle Kingdom.

Index

Abbott, E.C. ("Teddy Blue"), 43
Absentee owners, 80–84
Adams, Ramon, 64, 66
Adams, Steve, 112
Adams, Wess, 50
Allen, Poole, and Company, 27
Altgelt, Governor John P., 99
Antrim, Henry. *See* Billy the Kid
Archuleta, Judge J., 102
Archuleta County, Colorado, dispute, 100–104
Authentic Life of Billy the Kid. See Garrett, Pat

"Bad Men Cowboys, The." *See* Siringo, Charles A.
Barbed wire, 42; in Texas Panhandle, 17
Barrymore, Ethel, 113
Bass, Sam, 114
Bates, W.H. ("Deacon"), 53
Bates and Beals's LX Ranch, 53–78, 76, 114
Baufman, Theodore, 95
Bausman, Louis, 69, 71
Beals, David T. 50, 71, 78, 95
Benet, William Rose, 134
Betenson, Lula Parker: *Butch Cassidy, My Brother,* 127–28
Billy the Kid, 63–75, 95, 115 (Born Henry McCarty; later, Henry Antrim, alias William H. Bonney, alias Billy the Kid)
Bonney, William H. *See* Billy the Kid
Borah, William E., 112
Bowdre, Charlie, 73
Bowdre, Mrs. Charlie, 73
Brown, Henry, 95
Brown's Hole, Utah-Colorado-Wyoming, 115, 118
Buffalo herds, 51–52, 54–55
Bullion, Laura, 119, 126

Butch Cassidy and the Sundance Kid (movie), 115
Butch Cassidy, My Brother (Betenson, Lula Parker), 127–28

Carlyle, Jim, 70–71
Carver, Bill (Will), 119–26
Cattle Kingdom, The, 13, 21, 51, 79, 133
Cattle skinning, 33–35
Chambers, Lon, 67, 69, 73
Champion, Nathan, 118
Charles A. Siringo, A Texas Picaro. See Peavy, Charles D.
Chisholm, Jesse, 38–39
Chisholm Trail, 37–39
Chisum, Jinglebob John, 38, 73
Civil War in Texas, 24–25
Clark, Neil M., 132
Clifford, Frank ("Big-Foot Wallace"), 67, 72
Coghlin, Pat, 67, 71–72, 74–75
Cowboy Detective, A. See Siringo, Charles A.
"Cow hunt" in Gulf Coast country, 29–31; in the Texas Panhandle, 57–58
Cow "puncher," 60–61
Cowboy: "Bad man," 65; end-of-trail celebrations, 46–47, 49–50; equipment, 28–29, 56–57, 88; in big city, 61; Negro cowboy, 44, 135–36; origin of term "cowboy," 21–22; "tournament," 86–87
Cruzon, Bill, 126
Cully, John H., 118

Dale, E. E., 13
Dalhart, Vernon: "The Prisoner's Song," 129
Dalton Gang, 114

158